HOW TO WIN AN ARGUMENT

Surefire Strategies for Getting Your Point Across

Third Edition

Michael A. Gilbert

University Press of America,® Inc.
Lanham · Boulder · New York · Toronto · Plymouth, UK

Library of Congress Control Number: 2007942933
ISBN-13: 978-0-7618-4001-5 (paperback : alk. paper)
ISBN-10: 0-7618-4001-X (paperback : alk. paper)

To Zack,
who's always a winner

Table of Contents

Preface to the Third Edition

I learned how to argue on the streets of Flatbush, in Brooklyn, New York. Being a "good kid" and not a "hood," I had to do something to keep from having my head knocked off every day. So it was that I discovered the power of persuasive argument. Later, at Hunter College (now Lehman College) in the Bronx, small gangs of us used to hang out in the halls throwing trick questions at unsuspecting profs. But when I went straight and began teaching I was shocked to learn that very few people really knew how to listen and respond to an argument. Finally I had a mission: to make the world more critical.

This book is an important part of my mission, and as such it must be understandable to the average reader. (What good is a mission no one can understand?) So, in this revised edition I have maintained the ease of reading and comprehension so popular in the first edition. This book must be accessible because, if anything, it is even more important today that we all become adept at understanding and creating arguments. Demagoguery seems to be on the rise, and the media invade our minds with increasing skill and perseverance. Ever more we are presented with simplistic positions and addled argumentation. The world seems to be breaking up into opposing teams, and every team wants your allegiance. This book will enable you to choose wisely and carefully, and prevent you from being misled by fallacies and empty rhetoric. If I can increase your insight into and perception of the positions presented to you, if I can decrease your gullibility and replace it with a healthy scepticism, then I will have succeeded in doing something important.

The above words are from the original preface to the first edition, and they still hold for me today. I am extremely pleased that University press of America has agreed to re-issue *How To Win An Argument* in a third edition. Of all the work I have done in Argumentation Theory and Informal Logic, it is this book that seems to have had the greatest impact and stayed with my readers the most. I still encounter people who read the first edition almost twenty years ago who tell me how valuable they found it. I hope you will agree with them, and find, as they did, that your argument skills are improved by reading this book.

This third edition updates many examples, is re-written for greater comprehension, and includes more pointers and tips, (though there are a few old nuggets I could not bear to discard.) In addition, there is a completely new chapter on emotion that reflects the recent research I have been doing on interpersonal argumentation. The book does, however, keep the spirit and feeling of the original that was so popular with readers. Throughout the text you will find boxed statements. These are either brief summaries of important points, or tips for argument technique. They can serve as reminders and guides as you work through the material, and they will also serve as a quick refresher if you forget important elements. This revised edition also contains review exercises designed to insure that you understand the important points, and help you digest the material.

This book will show you how to argue and reason more effectively. It will also make you more aware of what is going on in an argument. So that you can actually see this happening, I urge you to begin by reading Part III and then to go back to Part I. Then when you read the whole book and go through Part III for the second time you can see your increased ability to identify flaws and fallacies. That will be your surety that the lessons learned in the book actually make a difference. This ability and your increased confidence can then be transferred to real arguments. All it takes is practice.

A great deal has changed in the academic field of Argumentation Theory since I wrote the first edition. In fact, the field barely existed back then. Now it is a thriving arena of scholarship with journals, conferences, courses, and competing approaches. Scholars from philosophy, communication theory, sociology and psychology work together to try and understand this most important of human activities. I want to thank my colleagues around the world for their encouragement and kind words about this book.

It's still true that I recruited a multitude of missionaries along the way, many of whom stayed with me and continue to help me. The impetus for the book came first from students in my courses and people at my talks and workshops, and this revised edition was urged upon me by many later students who felt cheated by *Win*'s unavailability. From them, the oldtimers and the newcomers, I culled examples and insights. Many spent time looking through newspapers and periodicals for juicy fallacies, and the book is richer for their contribution. Like any missionary I was often very zealous and obsessive—in short, annoying. To my many wonderful friends who put up with me, who read the book, and who have given me support and encouragement, I give my love. Finally, I would like to thank Lisa, Chris, Paul, Rachel, my wonderful wife Diane, and my son, Zachary to whom this revision is dedicated.

Michael A. Gilbert
Toronto, Canada
January 2007

Part I

THE ART OF ARGUMENT

1. What Are We Arguing About?

"I just don't want to argue about it."
"Don't argue with me."
"There's nothing to argue about, my mind is made up."
"Stop arguing and listen."

These expressions and others like them are thrown at us from childhood on. First, in our most tender years, we are just not allowed to argue. Later, in school, an arguer is often labeled "troublemaker" or, at the very least, "uncooperative." If we argue at work we are not "pulling with the team," or perhaps we are just "stubborn" and (still) "uncooperative." Lately, argument is not socially acceptable. We are not supposed to argue with people, instead we must be sympathetic, caring, and, above all, not hurt anyone's feelings. This is especially difficult when dealing with the argumentatively challenged. What is never clear is whether, after being politically careful, can we then challenge their arguments?

It is no wonder, with all this anti-argument propaganda, that most of us do it so poorly. And this is the real problem. It is not *argument* that is objectionable, but *bad* argument that puts everyone off. A good argument does show what someone's position is; it does allow others to present a point of view; it does help in reaching and understanding a decision; and it does not tread people helplessly underfoot. The purpose of this book is to teach you about good argument—how to win them, and how to experience the understanding, insight, and human contact that all good argument engenders.

Since very often the truth has little to do with winning or losing, the decision, even the knockout, may go to the sneakiest or slickest argument, and not to the best or wisest. It can be very frustrating to lose an argument from lack of expertise, experience, or confidence about *arguing*, and not because you were wrong. And if the outcome is important (perhaps a raise or promotion is at stake), your frustration will be that much greater as you tell yourself that you should have won that argument. You should have been able to make that point or defeat that objection.

But you did not.

What went wrong? What reply might have worked? What did you miss?

In the following example Our Hero is stymied. He is trying to persuade a clerk to give him both forms so he will not have to get on another line.

> OUR HERO: May I have a form for my driver's license renewal and a form of my car registration renewal, please?
>
> CLERK: Here's your license renewal; you get your registration renewal two lines to the left, over there.
>
> OUR HERO: Look, I've waited in this line for twenty minutes. All you have to do is reach over twelve inches and get me a registration form. Come on, be a sport. I don't want to wait on another line.
>
> CLERK: Sure. That's easy for you to say. But if I do it for you I'll have to do it for everybody. Then I'll be running all over the place getting all sorts of forms. How can I do my job if I'm always running around for different forms?

Instead of muttering under his breath and moving to the next line, Our Hero might have pointed out the weakness in the clerk's argument. Our Hero was not asking the clerk to run all over the place—only to reach twelve inches. As for the clerk's fear that she would have to do the same for everyone—why shouldn't she, if the task is so simple? There is no question of the clerk's having to desert her post. She can do it all right there, on the spot.

Our Hero and the clerk are, in the broadest sense, having an argument. Usually that word brings to mind violence, intensity, and a good deal of noise, shouting, and name-calling. Many arguments are indeed like that. But in this book I will use the word argument in a very broad way.

> **An argument is any disagreement—
> from the most polite discussion
> to the loudest brawl.**

So argument is a very broad word, including the many different methods people use in their attempts to persuade or convince. Simple informal discussions and disagreements are arguments. So are the debates and confrontations that precede fights, battles, and wars. Arguments can be among the mildest of polite conversations; and they can be the most violent and lethal exchanges. So long as two people are disagreeing *or think they are disagreeing*, they are having an argument.

Many people coming to take workshops from me complain that they become too emotional when they argue: they become excited and lose control, and in turn lose the argument. There is no reason why you should not become emotional and involved; in fact, it's virtually impossible not to be at least somewhat emotional. The trick is to use that emotion and involvement, not let it stand in the way of good arguing. Emotion is an integral part of arguing; after all, if you did not care about the topic, why argue at all?

Some people believe that arguments should always be crystal clear, unemotional, and devoid of drama and feeling. This view is wrong. An overly proper and correct argument is just like a very proper and correct party—a bore. Most arguments are not presented in prim and proper form; they are presented in any way that might be convincing. Besides, trying to make arguments behave according to textbook rules destroys them as an art form, as modes of expression and persuasion. The desire for carefully laid out arguments is understandable: the wish is to see arguments as careful, precise, beacons of reason. But who is so lucky? Day in and day out we read about or hear from those who make their livings by hoodwinking, cajoling, and fooling us (for example, politicians and advertisers.) They will not give up their bags of tricks simply because they hear a call to high moral standards. A far more promising hope is that the general public will arm itself with the skills of good argument. Then, if a politician commits a mistake in argument, he or she will be caught and embarrassed, and such shifty maneuvers are likely to decrease dramatically. Unlike arming people with guns or bombs, no one will die from being armed with the techniques of argument. Instead, real communication is increased through greater awareness of the complexities and subtleties of argument.

> **When it comes to argument -**
> **Knowledge is Power**

2. Why Argue So Much?

Why do we argue? Why do we make trouble? Why are we obnoxious and disagreeable? Why not just go along and not make waves? Because we are constantly faced with decisions. In order to make good decisions we have to consider the issues and the relevant arguments and positions. It is necessary to decide what issues are the most important, what topics the most vital.

Arguing provides the opportunity to explore and probe the claims and positions offered. In arguing you have a chance to examine exactly what your opposer's position rests upon. Plastic shopping bags should be made illegal. Why? What rights are involved? Who will suffer and who will gain? Are there alternatives to making the bags illegal? What problem forced this particular solution? What are the consequences of keeping them legal? When you argue you do not even have to disagree with a position in order to question it. By arguing you might just want to test or explore it the ideas presented. One major reason for arguing, then, is to learn: to explore, probe, and test in order to examine a belief.

Very often you argue when you already have a conviction, but want argue to persuade others. Sometimes you are the one being persuaded, at other times you are doing the persuading. It's around us all the time: others are always trying to persuade you. When the daily newspaper editorial supports compulsory garbage recycling and offers arguments, the aim is to convince us, the readers. The same holds for all arguments and positions presented on television and radio. In these situations you do not have the opportunity to reply. The argument is stated, and there it is, you can take it or leave it. You are presented with very polished and convincing arguments, but can't object.

Other forms of argument designed to persuade are the advertising messages that reach us by way of commercials, posters, jingles, and so on. The reasons presented for trying a product can be good, such as efficiency or low cost, or the reasons can be poor, such as prestige or an irrelevant endorsement. The errors in reasoning you find in advertising are the same as elsewhere. When Polly Politician says, "Unemployment may be reduced by as much as 22 percent in the next six months," she relies on the same "hedge-words" as an advertisement saying, "Shine toothpaste may reduce cavities by as much as 36 percent." Both use the expression "as much as," indicating only an outside possibility, and both use the word "may" instead of "will."

We often aim to convince someone of our view. If you suggest to a colleague who wants to open a new branch office that it might not be a good idea, you are arguing. He might, at the same time, be aiming to convince you that it is a good idea. In these situations you must be very quick. Someone presenting you with a position expects either assent or disagreement. If you disagree, then there is a responsibility to explain why. If you cannot come up with a reason for your objection, then you are expected to agree. This forms a basic principle of argument which will be discussed later.

Arguments can also be fun, especially when they are not about something too vital. Arguing is like playing, and it is not only possible, but desirable, to appreciate it on its own, without any desire to achieve some other end. Arguing when nothing is at stake can be a valuable experience, like playing a friendly game of tennis to prepare for a tournament. You'll be more at ease, and so can pay more attention to what you are saying and how you are saying it. You can take more risks on outrageous maneuvers, maybe try out a new shot.

You can also learn a lot about people from arguing with them. First, there is the obvious: you learn what they believe about the issue at hand and why they believe it. But, secondly, from the way they argue you also learn about their values, their beliefs, and the ways in which they present them. You end up not only with insights into your argument partner's *positions*, but into your partners as well.

> # When you argue
> # you examine your beliefs,
> # and learn about your partners
> # and yourself

A common old saying is that one should never argue about religion or politics. This is nonsense. You want your beliefs to be true, yet the adage warns us not to examine or test the most important and basic of them. Should these be left alone? No. These are just the beliefs that should be most carefully examined. By spotting weaknesses, mistakes, and falsehoods in your own and other people's arguments you stand a much better chance of holding and acting on true beliefs. The advantage of this is success: making decisions on false beliefs can only lead to error and trouble.

3. Kinds of Arguments

Arguments can be categorized in various ways, but one way deserves particular attention. This is the distinction between what I call "creative" and "attached" arguments. An argument is creative when the arguers are willing to explore a position in order to determine its value. This means you and your partner are willing to alter or reconsider a position if strong arguments are brought against it. An attached argument is just the opposite: you or your partner have a strong commitment to the position, there is an emotional or psychological stake in seeing one conclusion triumph. Many times this is understandable: you might, for example, be arguing for a raise or promotion and you want your point of view accepted, and that is all you care about.

Attachment to positions becomes a problem when there is real difference of opinion. Since attachment means the opposers are unwilling or unable to change their minds, they tend to get stubborn and uncooperative. They have no genuine desire to understand and deal with the opposing arguments. All that matters to them is holding onto their beliefs. No one enjoys having their beliefs knocked about, but most of the time we are willing to think about them and let them be probed. When an arguer cannot do this, then he is too attached to the belief. When you know that your opposer is very attached to some belief, you should treat the argument differently. If your opposer does not change her mind you should not assume you lost; sometimes *nothing* will change an opposer's mind. Arguing with a salesman about the value of his product, with a nationalist about the policies of her country, a parent about the beauty of his child—all are arguments that are not likely to end in agreement.

> **Watch out for
> strong attachment—
> both yours and your opposer's,
> and go slow when you find it.**

I ran into an example of strong attachment not long ago I was having a cappuccino at a local coffee bar. "You know," the owner told me, "I have the cheapest prices around."

"Well," I responded, "actually I stopped somewhere else yesterday, and he was cheaper by fifty cents."

"Oh," he said, "but what is the quality of the coffee? It's no bargain if the beans aren't the best."

This change of subject (from price to quality) told me as clearly as a flashing sign that the argument would go nowhere. Fortunately, I had no special interest in persuading the owner of anything.

If you are arguing with someone who is strongly attached to a position you cannot judge the outcome in the same way you judge a creative argument. Instead, you must carefully follow the line of reasoning in order to score for yourself, noting the weaknesses and strengths of all the arguments presented. The same holds if you are attached to a view. You might not want to publicly change your position at the time the argument is taking place, but you should try to carefully note the weak points of your own position to determine if they can be shored up, made sharper, or strengthened in some other way.

4. Defensive vs. Offensive Argument

The main thrust of this book is defensive. You will learn to defend yourself against bad arguments and tricky maneuvers. Many arguments, after all, do not require a response, since they come from the media and it is impossible to respond. So knowing how to defend yourself against the tricks is more valuable than being able to use them. But by continually identifying maneuvers and tricks, you will also learn how to use them to your own ends. By first learning how to defend, you will develop the skills needed to attack. I must caution you about using tricky maneuvers, however, because people who use dirty tricks often defeat their own purposes by acquiring a reputation which arouses suspicion.

> ## The essence of defensive argument is simple:
>
> *Assume everyone is out to get you!*

Most people you'll argue with want just one thing: agreement. And they do not care how they get it. If you believe this then you'll approach every argument with a very suspicious, critical, investigative attitude—and that s the first requirement for a successful arguer. *Believe nothing.* The less you believe, the less likely you are to believe something false. When arguing always assume your opposers are both sharp-minded and low-minded, so you'll never underrate their ability. Since many argument maneuvers are not made *consciously*, the simple fact that someone is sincere does not mean you can trust her arguments (though we might be able to trust the person). Many people think their arguments are correct when they are really full of errors. There are even those people who are so sure they are right that anything furthering their position is acceptable. This is the attitude that "the end justifies the means." But while they are already convinced, you should not be. You want the straight goods, while they want to sell you a bill of goods.

We all know how hard it is to probe for and discover the bad aspects of something we think we may want. Suppose you are considering moving into a new neighborhood. You might chat with several neighbors and ask them what they do not like about the area, but for many reasons this is difficult to do successfully. They are convinced that *when all is said and done* theirs is a good neighborhood to live in, while you want the data to make the very decision they have already made. But since they are firm in the belief that it is a good area, you won't get all the information from them.

Defensive techniques are especially fun when it comes to advertising. After a while you will cease to believe *anything* you see, read, or hear in an advertisement. Catch-words, hedge-words, unemphasized phrases abound throughout advertisements that seem to promise much, but in fact offer little. Often ads are designed to suggest certain associations or connections which are totally false. Sometimes it is sober looking men in suits designed to inspire confidence. At other times we are shown pictures of lovely men and women enjoying the very lifestyle we ourselves would like. Still others create an association with fun and youthful *bonhomie*. These associations are made and fostered very purposely.

A current fad in advertising relies on the public's concern for the environment. Suddenly products that were previously frowned upon are now being touted as 'green', and not harmful to the planet. Investigation shows that these claims are controversial, some even causing turmoil within environmental groups themselves. What is really going on? Have the products really been changed, or just the advertising? Are the manufacturers' and retailers' sudden concerns for the environment genuine, a marketing ploy, or both? The difficulty in answering such questions is obvious, but the point it that you must learn to be highly sceptical about *all claims* until the real proof is in.

> **There is no such thing as being too sceptical.**

After paying careful attention to arguments for a short period of time you will become trained to notice precisely what you are being told and precisely what you are reading. The exact claim made in an ad is often dramatically different from the claim that one might at first think is being made. Any time an ad claims to reduce your cost by as much as 23 per cent, you are supposed to be impressed. But this is just the maximum figure, and may well be a fluke or fairly rare occurrence. The point is this: the more suspicious you are, the less likely you are to be hoodwinked.

5. Some Warnings

When arguments are conducted properly they increase contact between people and afford a healthy form of interaction. But not all arguments are conducted properly: attachment often leads quickly to a loss of perspective and calm. Sometimes, too, it is not what the argument is about but whom the argument is with that is the cause of attachment. Arguing with any psychological rival—such as one's boss, teenage son, spouse, or colleague—can lead to heated argument not because of the subject but because of the people arguing and their relationship to each other. We are all familiar with fights between married couples or children and parents that were really about "nothing." The ostensible reason for the fight or argument hides a deeper issue. In these situations it is especially important to be very careful that winning not be seen as coming out on top. It is also terribly important to argue as creatively as possible, constantly leaving yourself open to hear your opposer's words and position.

In general, learn to judge how attached your opposer is to the position. Also try to note how attached he or she is to winning. Some people do not especially care how they come out of an argument, but will still defend their position as best they can. Others seem to have a need to come out victorious. In all these situations try to judge just what you will get from pushing hard, and what the cost might be to your opposer. In short, it is sometimes better to back off than attack.

> **If an opposer**
> **is very attached to a position**
> **and you are not, back off.**
>
> **It's not worth it.**

If your opposer is very attached to a position you will rarely get her to change her basic view. But going at it in little bits and pieces, one move at a time, you may make slower but deeper progress. This means you may not make progress all at once, but over time and by paying careful attention to the details of the arguments, you may see your opposer change her position.

This is a good time to raise another warning. Most of us have one or two issues on which we are inflexible. There may be one or two (hopefully not more) subjects on which you have an opinion and will never really budge. What is more, every time you get into an argument on one of these topics you argue very poorly and end up very irritated. This happens to all of us. The topics can be anything. Frequently they are themes with which we were raised. It might have to do with the liberation of the ancestral home. Basques discussing Spain, Estonians on Russians, or Jews and Palestinians on Israel often find it hard to be dispassionate. It seems as if too much is at stake. While it does not mean they are wrong, it does mean the issue is so emotionally alive for them they cannot discuss it coolly, and may even have difficulty being reasonable. Most of us have blind spots such as these.

Come to know your blind spots, and when you are incapable of arguing reasonably know that it is time to stop. If you maintain a position largely because of your upbringing or emotional involvement, how can you truly argue? Your reason for arguing will basically be that you want to believe in this thing, and no one is going to change your mind. But what kind of a reason is that? Things are not true simply because we want them to be. So, you may not be able to present good reasons for the position, and will not be able to tolerate those reasons being probed.

Again, the best thing to do in these cases is to back off. The only difficulty, of course, is the effect the position may have on others. If the belief involves others—if it touches on issues such as abortion or racial prejudices for example —then there is a responsibility to investigate. So the answer seems to lie in being aware of our blind spots while at the same time trying, perhaps gently, to explore them. If you are careful and do not go beyond the point of risk or irritation you may learn a great deal. And as you learn, the point of risk or irritation will become clearer; you will develop a finer sense of your own blind spots and perhaps begin to examine them critically.

The rule is to remember that your chances of changing someone's mind when they are deeply attached to a position are slight. So it makes sense to just try and make a dent in their position by slow and careful exploration. If you can't change someone's mind, then at least try to sow doubts; then at the next encounter you can try and move further.

One last warning is in order. The techniques in this book are fairly powerful. By the time you've finished this book you'll find it is easy, at the very least, to confuse people who are not on guard. Don't do it. The techniques in the pages that follow are presented to give you a better idea of what you are up against. But by learning how you can be deceived you also learn how to deceive. You can combat the would-be deceivers by pointing up their deceptions. But if you yourself turn to deception, we are just increasing the number of deceivers. Socrates, remember, was put to death for (allegedly) making the worse argument seem the better, and the better argument seem the worse. The worst you might do is to be obnoxious, and even though the penalties today are not nearly so severe, the temptation will be there.

> **Remember:**
> **Don't be obnoxious!**

6. Super-Rule I: Never Admit Defeat

I've been talking all along about winning arguments. But what, after all, does it mean to win an argument? Mostly we think of our opposer capitulating, giving in, and accepting our position: "Gadzooks, you're right! And all this time I was wrong. Thank you for showing me the light." Oh yes, sweet victory. But this hardly ever happens.

The topic under debate in part determines what winning means in any particular argument. If, for example, you are arguing about a yes-or-no situation then in many cases the winner can be easily identified. If you are arguing about opening a branch office and it is in the end opened, the person who wanted it opened is the victor. But even in such a seemingly clear case as this there may be compromises which mean that there really was no crystal-clear winner.

Usually when you argue you do not get the sort of turn-about you might like. What you can often do, however, is to plant seeds of doubt in the mind of your opposer, shaking the foundations of his position or belief. Sometimes you might return weeks later to find your opposer has completely changed positions. And, while she may never be admit it, the change is likely due to the argument.

If an argument is creative, then in one very important sense no one loses. A creative argument involves people who have a belief or hunch or idea about the truth, but who are also open to change. So the result of the argument will either confirm one particular view or show that it is not correct. In either case you leave this kind of argument with more information than you had before. If you are not swayed, then you know at least that these particular arguments were not effective enough. On the other hand, your opposer may have planted seeds of doubt, or pointed out new difficulties in your argument, and this too is valuable.

> **No one really loses
> a creative argument.**

Often in a creative argument neither position is a clear victor, yet the investigation, the examination of the issues and problems, provides insights and information about the position. This means that you always come out ahead, which is one very important kind of winning.

Here is a very important question that may come up in the course of an argument when you realize you are wrong. Your opposer has presented aspects of the problem you have not thought of, and at this time you cannot think of any reasonable reply. What should you do? Admit defeat and change the position? Admit that you cannot answer these points? Or should you use some maneuver that will cover your tracks and get yourself out of the argument? This is a very important question, and the answer, Super-Rule I, is controversial.

Super-Rule I

Never admit defeat unless you are absolutely convinced, and even then keep your mouth shut and wait till Monday.

Super-Rule1 rule means that you should never hastily concede defeat except in circumstances necessary to your well-being (to keep your job or save your marriage, for example). It is possible to admit defeat later, but at the time of argument it is almost always inappropriate to concede.

The defense of Super-Rule I is very simple. In the vast majority of cases we are not arguing about matters of fact, but about matters of opinion or value. If the argument is about a matter of fact it may be simply decided: There is an answer. When arguing about the capital of Saskatchewan, or the author of *For Whom the Bell Tolls*, for example, there is no need to continue once you check the right source. Popping onto the Internet for a few minutes will simply settle the matters. But most arguments are about matters of opinion. What is the best car to buy today? Is this a good time to expand our sales operations? Should Emma be allowed to watch so much television? These questions do not have straightforward answers. Even experts would not agree. So one opinion has as much initial possibility of being correct as any other. The purpose of these arguments is to determine which side can hold up better under examination.

If the purpose of the argument is to investigate a view under fire, to explore a position when it is being pushed to its limits, then what is the value of giving up? When someone concedes defeat the exploration stops. When that happens, the winner will cease considering the argument seriously and hearing the objections to the attack, and instead just savor the victory. So one reason for Super-Rule I is the desire to keep the investigation open.

A second reason for Super-Rule I lies in our own limitations. We are each familiar with the jolt of thinking what we should have said, but usually when you think of that perfect sparkling reply it is too late. Admitting defeat requires a good deal of faith in your ability to think of all the reasonable replies. There is absolutely nothing wrong with saying, "That's an interesting point. I am going to stop now, but assure you that I will consider your argument further." Schopenhauer wrote, in "The Art of Controversy,"

> The argument which would have been our salvation did not occur to us at the moment. Hence we make it a rule to attack a counter-argument, even though to all appearances it is true and forcible, in the belief that its truth is only superficial, and that in the course of the dispute another argument will occur to us by which we may upset it, or succeed in confirming the truth of our statement. [Arthur Schopenhaur, "The Art of Controversy"]

It is perfectly possible that what seems clear and convincing to you at this moment may not seem so credible later on. Not admitting defeat leaves open the possibility of continuing discussion.

Some will say this attitude is unreasonable. It is a cautious attitude, but I do not believe it is unreasonable. A good, thorough argument takes careful thought and a lot of time. Rarely do we allow the time an argument really requires. If you admit defeat quickly you are liable to be both mistaken and eventually change your mind. The responsibility is on you to think of the replies you need, or to finally agree to change your mind, but you need the time and context in which to do this properly. If you take losing an argument seriously, then losing means really changing your mind and you should not give up easily. By not conceding hastily you are giving your capitulation more respect and meaning.

> **A quick win is often
> not durable.**

You may find that many of those with whom you argue are better persuaders, speakers, and arguers than you are. They may also be attached to their positions and willing to persuade you at all costs. To admit defeat as a result of an argument with such a person is unilateral disarmament. There are people out there who want to persuade you of all sorts of silly things, so you must adopt a healthy critical stance to protect yourself from the tremendous amounts of hogwash constantly thrown at you.

Like anything else in this book, Super-Rule I does not apply across the board. I could perhaps say that there is a **Super-Rule O: No Rule Applies All the Time**. But this is something that should go without saying. Sometimes you may realize you have simply made a mistake in reasoning. You may, for example, have thought your opposer's position on abortion implied that no killing was ever justified, but she clearly pointed out why that is not the case. In this kind of situation there is nothing wrong with retracting an objection. Caution should not be confused with pigheadedness.

7. How Are Arguments Built?

The preliminaries are over and it is time to get down to work. We always argue, one hopes, about something: "We should expand the plant," or, "When all is said and done we're still better off with a small car," or, "Jimmy is much too young to go on an overnight trip without supervision," and so on. Arguments will surround these statements. Reasons will be given why they should be accepted or rejected. What's even more confusing is that you have to argue about the reasons. The statement describing the argument is the claim. It is usually stated at the outset and it identifies the topic of the argument. The claim is what the argument is about.

It is amazing how often people do not know what an argument is about. This is not only true of marital disputes running on more than one level, but also of less attached arguments. Frequently people are confused by an opposer's statements into following some track that leads in a completely wrong direction. If asked why they were bringing in some particular point they would have no reply. It is like a swiftly running racehorse who turns off the course and onto a driveway: he is still running, but not in the race. This happens so frequently that I present the following rule.

> **Always know
> what you are arguing about.**

This may seem like a silly rule, but what is silly is that we need such a rule, and experience shows the rule itself is essential.

It is very easy to find out what the argument is about: Ask. This is a good idea since then you find out what you want to know, and also get the opposer's statement of the claim. Such a step provides crucial information: how is your opposer viewing the argument? When his claim is carefully stated you can then recall what you think the argument was about. The differences between what you think and what she thinks can be very important.

> **A very good way of getting out of an argument you seem to be losing is to ask something like, "What do you think we are arguing about?"**
>
> **Whatever answer is returned say, "Oh, I see. I thought you meant something else."**

Another advantage to asking is that you gain time because your opposer has to formulate an answer. Sometimes you might even ask just to get some time to think. If you're confused you can always ask to have the topic restated. Sometimes your opposer will have no trouble providing an immediate, terse, correct statement of the claim. But more often, she too will be confused and will have to think. This all provides time for us to marshal a counter-argument.

> **Should someone ask you to state the claim, especially if there is an audience, say, "I had a feeling you didn't know what we were arguing about. Why don't *you* try taking a guess?"**

While the claim is the topic and focus of the argument, most of the time will be spent on the reasons for accepting or rejecting the claim. Every claim must be supported by reasons. Reasons answer the question, "Why accept this claim?" If good reasons cannot be effectively attacked , you must accept the claim. This is a basic key to understanding arguments: if the reasons are good and the logic is correct, you are bound to accept the claim. This is why you never attack claims directly. If Paul and Kelly are arguing about what sort of car to buy, there is no value in each of them just stating and re-stating a claim. Paul wants to dismiss Kelly's reasons for buying a sports car: "They are not cheaper to own even though they are good on gas," he might argue, "since they are expensive to service." Simply saying, "I don't want a sports car," makes clear what the argument is about, but is not persuasive.

Reasons are usually, but not always, the focus of an argument. Sometimes there is nothing wrong with the reasons, but the logic is not correct, the claim just does not follow. Suppose that Greene is a cruel murderer. Maya's opposer says, "There is no doubt that Greene is the killer. Let's hang the crumb."

"Well, I agree," Maya may say, "that Greene is the killer. But I can't agree that he should be hanged; that does not follow." Even though Maya agrees Greene is guilty, she points out that her opposer has not established the claim. It just does not follow only from what her opposer said that Greene should be killed; more argument is required.

> # Always attack the reasons for a claim,
> # not the claim itself.

When you provide a reason to back up a claim it must always be defended. "We should get a sports car because they are easier to maintain," is a reason that supports the claim, buy a sports car. When your opposer says, "What makes you think that sports cars are cheaper to maintain?" then that reason has been attacked and so you must defend it.

"They are cheaper on gas because most have four-cylinder engines." This last comment is a reason for the reason. While this can go on forever, most arguments are self-limiting. Sometimes you reach a point of common knowledge or agreement, while other times you may reach a point of fundamental disagreement. Learning what the crucial matters about which you and your opposer disagree is valuable. Once this is known, the chances of reaching some consensus can be judged. How basic is the difference? Is it an irreconcilable difference? These are important questions.

8. The Principle of Rationality

The Principle of Rationality

We always assume
people have reasons
for their beliefs.

Someone who believes something without reason is being irrational. In terms of argument, being rational means providing reasons for beliefs. In the end we may all be irrational, since sooner or later we reach the point of ultimate beliefs, where it is sometimes impossible to provide reasons. But at other times it is surprising how, with some thought and prodding, we can often go beyond even ultimate principles and provide rationales. The sequence of beliefs and reasons probably comes back and meets itself, so that in the end beliefs form a circle.

Your willingness to argue with other people rests on the Principle of Rationality. I assume that if you believe something you have a reason, and you assume the same for me. The following sort of dialogue does not occur:

"Lets get a sports car."

"Why?"

"No reason."

Your initial reaction on hearing this argument would simply be disbelief: there must be reason. It may be a silly reason, but a reason nonetheless, otherwise why want a sports car at all? (People who do things without reason often find themselves under medical scrutiny.) The Principle of Rationality is necessary to argument since there is no point in arguing with someone who does not have reasons. The assumption is that you must always defend your positions and actions on request. Without this assumption communication and argument would come to a halt.

Now, mind you, the Principle of Rationality states you will be given reasons for position, but it says nothing about their quality. There is no guarantee you will be given good reasons. They may be whatever was thought of first:

"Why are you going to vote for Stevens?"

"Because my cousin went to high school with his sister."

That is hardly a good reason for wanting someone in office, but it satisfies the principle. The principle does not claim you will be given the opposer's true reasons or motivation:

"Why do you want to be president, Mr. Jarvis?"

"Solely to serve my country."

Jarvis probably has other interests as well, but he need not present them to comply with the principle. The real reasons for wanting to be president or wanting to buy a sports car may have nothing to do with the reasons stated. A desire for a sports car rarely has very much to do with economy and careful decision making. But arguers often hide their real reasons behind some other, less embarrassing, reasons. This is called rationalization, and it shows how basic the Principle of Rationality is. We always want to give reasons, and if we do not like the real reasons we'll will make up others.

One sort of person often lacking reasons is a fanatic. There are two rules of dealing with a fanatic.

First Rule For Dealing With a Fanatic:

Don't.

But we all succumb to temptation. Fanatics are so easy to rile and excite that the desire to argue with them is often overwhelming. If you do proceed, there are two points to keep in mind. The first is that fanatics can provide useful information. Frequently they are quite well informed about their subject and can offer every standard argument. They tend not to go very deep, but they do frequently have an excellent grasp of the basic arguments. The second point is to appreciate the standard fanatic's argument. Generally, the argument will run somewhat as follows. For this example, let's suppose our fanatic is a "triadist" (whatever it is). (Let Triadism stand for your favorite fanatic's position.)

FANNY FANATIC: Triads are the essence of the universe. Everything comes in triples.

OUR HERO: What on earth does that mean?

FANNY: To properly understand the universe you must see the triads.

OUR HERO: How can I see them? I don't off-hand see anything that might be a triad.

FANNY: Ah....First you must learn to look and truly *see* the world.

OUR HERO: How do you know that the way you see the world is the "true" way?

FANNY: I know. Once you see it, you too will know.

OUR HERO: I disagree. I don't see anything and think there's probably nothing else to see.

FANNY: That is only because your vision is clouded.

OUR HERO: How do you know your vision is not clouded?

FANNY: Oh, I know. I know.

Nothing will move Fanny. She is relying on a fallacy called "special pleading." She is claiming knowledge which is privileged: it is available to her only. Anyone who disagrees with her is blind in some way. There is nowhere to go with the argument, since nothing will be accepted by a fanatic as evidence against the position. This leads to our second rule: ask Fanny what would prove she is wrong. If the answer is that nothing could prove her wrong, then give up. (This maneuver is good for any very stubborn opposer who seems unwilling to discuss reasons.)

Second Rule For Dealing With a Fanatic:

When stuck, ask, "What would it take to prove you are wrong?"

Progress may not be made, but at least you can say you tried. Fanny might reply to the question by saying that if anything vital was shown to come in a pair instead of a triad then she would have to reconsider. The difficulty then would be to find an acceptable pair. A good fanatic will be expert in showing why particular bits of counter-evidence are not relevant. Pointing out a pair like Love-Hate would undoubtedly bring the response that you have misconstrued the relationship, it's really Love-Neutrality-Hate. (What is terribly interesting, but not to Fanny, is that pairism is every bit as easy to defend as triadism.)

The Principle of Rationality is vital to argument because it gives you something to attack. If the reasons are not good or real they will probably not stand up very well. As they are dismissed you may get closer to the truth. So even when the reasons are poor you can make progress.

9. Two More Principles

One of the major assumptions we all make about our beliefs and positions is that we have reasons for them. There is another assumption every bit as general and every bit as important. In its simplest guise the assumption is that an arguer will be consistent. Without this assumption all argument would grind to a very sudden halt. Remember the motor-vehicle office clerk in Chapter 1: part of the argument he offered Our Hero was the need to apply a rule in all cases. The clerk was concerned that if he obtained a registration form for Our Hero he would have to get it for everyone. Consistency demands that we have a reason for making exceptions, for distinguishing in similar cases. If there are three children and you give them each a prize, no explanation is called for. But if you give just one a prize, then you must account for the difference. This might be very easy: the prize might have gone to the winner of a contest or to the best behaved. Whatever the reason, regardless of whether it is a good reason or a bad reason, we expect one. Imagine a woman on the line at the motor-vehicle office who sees Our Hero in front receiving two forms. This woman's turn comes, and she asks for the same two forms and is refused. She would demand an explanation, and if none were forthcoming would likely raise a horrible fuss. If everybody but one in an office received a raise, an explanation would also be sought. What is wanted is the relevant difference between the two cases.

One notorious example where a relevant difference becomes crucial is in arguments about abortion. One of the arguments offered by those against abortion is that there is no relevant difference between a fetus and a newborn baby. If this is so, then what applies to one must apply to the other. Since killing babies is acknowledged by practically everybody as immoral, a supporter of abortion must find a relevant difference between a fetus and a baby. In other words, if a fetus has the same rights as a baby we cannot simply kill it. (Nor could we put a pregnant woman in prison, but that's another story.) Needless to say, the sides do not agree on the relevant differences, but both sides agree on the importance of a relevant difference.

Another example concerns the F.B.I.: none of us are allowed to do any number of things the F.B.I. has done. Over the years, this has included sending fake threatening letters, illegal wiretapping and general harassment. When approached the F.B.I. has usually offered their function as guardians of security as providing the relevant difference between the restriction on our behavior and the lack of restrictions on theirs. Sometimes, depending on the political mood of the times, the U.S. Congress and courts have rejected the importance of this distinction.

I shall express this need for pointing out differences in the next principle:

The Principle of Similar Cases

**Where two cases or situations are similar,
a reason must be offered
for not treating them the
same.**

This principle goes very nicely with the Principle of Rationality. The first principle states that you will be given reasons for beliefs and positions presented to you. The new one makes it clear that beliefs about which things are the same and which are different falls under the Principle of Rationality. Consider an argument about a stop light. At a meeting of the local neighborhood association a City Councilman is trying to make her case:

> OUR HERO: We need a stop light at this corner. Children cross there all the time, and one of them is going to get hurt.
> COUNCILMAN: That intersection is identical to hundreds of others in the city. Why should we put a light there and not at the others?
> OUR HERO: This one is more dangerous than most.
> COUNCILMAN: No it's not. There have been fewer accidents at this intersection than at many others which do not have lights.

The Councilman is appealing to the Principle of Similar Cases. Why should this intersection be singled out? In such a situation there are only two choices for Our Hero. He can maintain that there is a difference and make a position for it, or he can agree that there is no difference. If he agrees that there is no difference, his best move is to maintain that *all* these intersections should have lights. So the argument might continue in one of two ways. The first is as follows:

> OUR HERO: Of course, I'm sure you're right. What we believe is that *all* of these intersections should have lights. And we want to know what you are going to do about it!

These arguments also utilize the third and final principle:

The Principle Principle

Virtually every position can be expressed in terms of a general principle:

for everything there is a principle.

When the Councilman was told that a stop light was wanted she immediately drew out the implicit principle or rule: put stop lights in dangerous intersections. Knowing the rule Our Hero is committed to it, (after all, it is his rule), the Councilman can argue against it. She might point out that it is too expensive, that it would slow traffic too much, and so on. By extracting the principle she now has a handle on what she is fighting about.

Virtually every argument can be seen as one or both of two things. First, an argument about the truth of some principle; or, second, an argument about the application of some principle. It is not always easy to know what principles are at issue, but it is always important.

> **Always know the principles to which
> you are committed,
> and always know the principles to which
> your opposer is committed.**

In many jurisdictions there is a great deal of controversy concerning making the use of motorcycle and/or bicycle helmets compulsory. The greatest objection to this legislation is directed to the underlying principle that an individual's safety is not a proper object of legislation. The argument may center on whether or not this principle is true. But, on the other hand, the argument may concern whether or not this principle applies. To show this you might argue that it is not personal safety, but the effect on others (through increased hospital costs, lost work hours and so on,) that warrants the legislation. Now the principle concerns communal cost, not interference with personal freedom, so the principle that our freedom should not be curtailed without reason has not been violated.

Suppose we want to attack the new principle. The Principle of Similar Cases states that cases which appear the same must be treated the same. The new rule says that a practice that will lower communal costs may be required by legislation. So, you might ask your opposer, what about compulsory exercise? Is compulsory exercise the same as wearing a bike helmet? Why not? If it is, your opposer must accept that position or give up the principle.

Always identify your opposers' principles. By looking at their positions and reasons you can figure out what the principle is. Just knowing that your opposer is against mandatory helmet legislation is not enough. But when you know he is against it *because* it interferes with personal liberty you can determine the principle: personal liberty should not be curtailed. A person who is against abortion because it cheapens life holds a principle different from a person who is against abortion because God forbids it. While the position is the same, the reasons are different. The first opposer is committed to the principle that what cheapens life is wrong. The second opposer believes the rule that what God commands should be obeyed. We would expect the first to be against war, while the second would have to consult religious authorities.

Identifying your opposer's principle is the first step. The second is finding good examples. A good example is one that fits the principle but is rejected by your opposer. Suppose your opposer favors compulsory helmet use because it cuts down on communal costs. The example involving compulsory exercise is a good one: if we all had to work out or jog communal hospital costs would go down, so the principle applies. But few people would want to support compulsory exercise legislation, so a difference must be found between helmet wearing and exercise. If it is not found, the principle must be changed: the principle leads to both helmet wearing and exercise—so the principle must go. On the other hand, if your opposer is willing to accept compulsory exercise the principle stays, and you have to look for a different example.

The last option is for your opposer to find a difference between the two. Perhaps bicycling is a privilege, while not having to exercise is a right. In this case the principle does not lead to both cases, so there is no problem for your opposer. Again, we look for a different example.

Suppose we were arguing against any sexual discrimination in hiring. Your principle is that anyone qualified for a job should be able to get it. Your opposer is trying to come up with examples where we would not want to apply the Principle of Similar Cases. He might try to stymie you with: "What about women football players? Should women be able to try out for the defensive line of the Giants?" If you say, no, you must give up the principle or say why this case is different. But, since you pay attention to your arguments and you know what principles you are committed to, you are not thrown off your pace by his counter-example of women football players: "Sure," you reply, "if they can compete, more power to them. They ought to be able to try. There's already been at least one woman in professional hockey player. I don't know if a woman would make it in football, but that's not the point. It's the opportunity, not the job, that concerns me." A general rule is appropriate at this point:

> **Whenever possible,**
> **embrace the consequences**
> **of your position.**

This means you are better off accepting the odd consequences you may not have anticipated rather than changing the principle. Arguing that the examples are not similar or changing the principle can be dangerous. If the example can be dismissed as different, there is no problem. But if not, try to hold onto the principle by accepting the example.

10. Super-Rule II: Listen!

There is one more Super-Rule to be presented. This rule should never be forgotten or neglected. Failure to pay attention to it leads to disaster.

```
Super-Rule II

Listen!
```

People rarely listen to each other. Most of the time when you should be listening, you are doing something else, like thinking of what you are going to say next, or trying to remember if you defrosted anything for dinner. Everyone has had the experience of explaining a position or belief to someone very carefully only to realize they have not heard a word. This, above all else, is the most difficult obstacle to effective communication in argument: Failure to listen.

The value of listening carefully cannot be overemphasized. In the first place the shock value alone will stand you in good stead. Instead of the usual "you say your piece—now I say mine—now you say yours" and so on, (something I call simultaneous monologues,) you need to pay attention. Many people step back in astonishment at the realization that it is *their argument* which is being addressed, and not just your next random thought. Returning with a comment indicating that you heard your opposer was heard will have great effect; sometimes the sheer surprise will throw your opposer off balance.

In normal conversation listening is nice, but not critical. In many conversations, like the following one, it is not even expected:

CHRIS: I just got a new car. A jeep.
PAUL: Oh, yeah. They're great. I had one about eight years ago.

CHRIS: I got a great price on it. The owner is going abroad.

PAUL: Mine was a hand-me-down from a cousin, believe it or not.

CHRIS: It's amazing on dirt, just goes anywhere. Last week we drove right up a half-mile hill on bare rock.

PAUL: Yeah. I remember taking mine out to the beach all the time....

There is nothing wrong with this conversation. Chris and Paul want a chance to talk about their respective jeeps. There is no special need to listen. Paul will fondly reminisce while Chris excitedly talks about his new car. Conversations about cars, holidays, movies, books, and so on are often the same. We do not listen because we are not really interested and nothing is at stake. At the same time the participants each get to tell some stories and chat a bit, which is what they really want to do.

When it comes to having an argument the situation changes. It is impossible to really persuade someone who has an opinion without listening to him or her very carefully. By listening to the arguments you are able to attack and discuss the reasons presented to you. And only by showing that the arguments do not work can you win. The same holds if you are defending a position. Unless you can show that your opposer's objections are wrong you will not convince her. If you meet her every objection you might make some progress. Both attacking an argument and defending a position require that you pay careful attention to what is being said. Arguing without listening is like driving with tunnel-vision: You can only see where you are going, not where anyone else is.

> **Listening provides the fuel
> for the engine of
> argument.**

Knowing the rules and gambits of argument is important, but it is impossible to use these tools if you are not listening. It is a rare argument that does not contain some mistake or weak point, but you will only notice it if you are listening when it comes. The world's greatest non-listener to date was a teacher I encountered at a parents' meeting not long ago. This amazing individual, in charge of the meeting, was quite agitated and upset that no parent had volunteered to help supervise activities next Monday. We were being harangued and exhorted. It took three people about six attempts to get through the information that there was no school next Monday. (I shuddered to think how the children fared in his classroom.)

Dealing with hard-core non-listeners is difficult. Everyone fails to listen sometimes. You might get excited or abstracted and not be paying as much attention as usual. But some people find it almost impossible to listen. In these cases repetition is the only thing that works. Unless your opposer is terribly long winded, do not interrupt; wait patiently until she has finished and then politely say, "I'm sorry. You did not hear my point. Let me try again...." This may not work. Your opposer will once again go off on a little trip of her own without paying the slightest heed to your comments. Now you interrupt, apologize, and say something like, "You're missing my point. Look, you said...then I said...So you now must explain how you will deal with my objection."

> **The only way to deal with a
> non-listener is
> with patience and repetition.**

Even this last attempt may fail. But take solace: the true non-listener suffers a lonely fate—no one wants to talk to him.

11. Emotional Turmoil

One of the constant struggles we face when arguing about something close to home or with someone close to home is keeping our emotions in check. But before we start bad mouthing emotions, we must realize that *all arguments are emotional.*

> **There is no such thing
> as a non-emotional argument.**

Anytime we are moved to argue, it is because we care about the matter at hand. There is something in it that, at the least, grabs our attention enough to move us to disagree. This is emotion. The emotions may not be strong or play a significant factor, but they are there. Always.

Sometimes the presence of emotion is very obvious, and we can feel ourselves becoming emotional. We might sense anger, frustration, impatience, disappointment, or joy, eagerness, or excitement beginning to increase. This is absolutely fine. There is nothing wrong with feeling emotional, even feeling very emotional. It is only when our emotions begin to interfere with our ability to make and listen to arguments that there is a problem. Being emotional is never a problem, but being over-emotional is. So, what do we do when we feel that emotions are taking over and we are losing control? Why, stop arguing.

> ## If you feel you cannot
> ## control your emotions,
>
> ## withdraw from the argument.

Saying that you need a moment, or that you have to think, is all that ought be necessary in order to have a break. When you do break, try and think why you are reacting the way you are, and what you might do about it. Is some nerve being touched? Is it a "hot spot" or trigger point we are aware of? Something we're particularly sensitive about? Or, is this new information that we need to process? In either case, the break should provide a chance to review the situation and bring yourself under control. The situation may not, however, call for a real break. Sometimes just taking a few breaths to compose yourself is sufficient.

The most common emotional experience occurring within arguments is anger. Whether because of something that was said, or the way the argument is proceeding, or from a feeling of helplessness, we notice anger rising within us. Generally, *anger increases when one of the partners to the dispute is not feeling heard.* Not feeling heard is not the only reason for anger, but it is the most common one. So, if you feel yourself becoming irritated, check out if you feel that your arguments are not being taken seriously or are being misunderstood. If that is the root cause, then try a different approach.

> ## If your words
> ## are not being heard,
> ## try different words.

By trying a different approach you may be able to get through to your partner where you were having trouble before. It also provides you with breathing room. In short, if you feel your anger rising, don't just try to quash it; use it as a guide to signal yourself that things are not going well.

Far from being ruinous, emotion and its display can be a powerful tool in an argument. When I ask my students, especially the women, if they ever use emotion in the form, say, of tears to help in an argument, they look at me as if to say, "Duh? Of course we do." Now, you don't want to go about crying in front of your supervisors, or have a full blown tantrum with your friends or family. But showing your emotions, letting your opposer see how much you care about the issue can be both useful and important for both of you. Someone being cavalier in an argument might re-think that attitude if she sees how you are feeling about the issue. Someone who is not terribly attached to the outcome might even back off if you demonstrate that it means a lot to you.

We need also to consider the opposite side of the coin. What about arguing with someone who is emotional? Well, obviously, the first question is, how emotional? We know that emotion is always present when we argue, so we can't really expect to argue with someone and not experience their emotions. In fact, we need to be tolerant of emotions; even to the point of offering a break if it seems called for. Remember what was said above: the most common reason for anger is the feeling of not being heard, the sense that your position is not understood. If someone with whom you are arguing starts to become angry, then perhaps she is not feeling like you understand her arguments. This might be a good moment for you to ask for a re-cap.

> Emma: So, that's why your plan won't work. It's against the rules.
> Our Hero: Then why can't they just change the rule?
> Emma: [showing some heat] Oh, come on! They can't just change them for you.
> Our Hero: Hey, hang on. I'm missing something. Can you back up and lead me through this again?

Our Hero, seeing things are not going well, wants to give himself another chance to understand Emma's argument. He knows that understanding a partner's argument is the single most important key to successful disputing. Whether he ends up agreeing or disagreeing, he must understand Emma's position in order to either concur or try to change her mind. Her display of emotion means he was not succeeding, so he is trying something different.

Emotion can, and sometimes will, get out of hand, and then an argument may degenerate into a quarrel. We can avoid those situations by expecting emotion, paying attention to it, and respecting it.

12. Scoring a Goal

Listening when we are arguing with someone is a central and important habit. We must cultivate the technique and train our ears to pick up important information and vital cues. But, we might fairly ask, "What information and what cues?"

Well, first of all, there is the *information* your opposer is using. What data is she bringing forward to bolster her position? Is it trustworthy? Is it correct? Up to date? And always remember, when an opposer uses a source of information you can also tap that source. What about the *reasons* being brought forth? Can you use them? Do they make sense to you? Do the data and the reasons actually support the conclusion?

These are all questions that the previous chapters can help you answer. There is, however, one further sort of information and cues that have not yet been mentioned. These are your opposer's *goals*. Exactly what does he hope to achieve in this discussion? Why is he arguing with you? What, really, does he want?

> **Listen for information,
> listen for reasons,**
>
> **but above all listen for
> *goals*.**

Goals are a lot more complex than we usually think they are. There's the obvious goal of winning the argument and getting what you want. Little Jimmy should go to sleep away camp, or Dawn should head up the Claxco project, and so on. But often the goals we think we have are not the only ones around. If we look deeper and think more, explore the territory, we might see that there are others we might even be happy with. Watch as Our Hero settles a dispute with Natalie.

> Olivia: I'm really convinced that Dawn should get the Claxco project. She's been waiting for a break for a long time, and I think she's ready for a challenge.
>
> Our Hero: Really? The Claxco project is a very technical one, and that doesn't strike me as Dawn's forte.
>
> Olivia: I'm sure she can handle it. After all, she'll have a team supporting her.
>
> Our Hero: I think she might be better off with the Wesbot account.
>
> Olivia: But it's not as big. She deserves something big.
>
> Our Hero: Well, it's not as big, but it's certainly not little. And, she'd have a much better chance of coming out a star with an account she can relate to more easily. That's what you want, after all, isn't it?
>
> Olivia; Him, you do have a point there...

Our Hero saw that Olivia's goal was bringing Dawn up the ladder. When he realized this he was able to offer an alternate solution that met her goal, but satisfied his own. That cannot happen unless we are listening and paying attention to what our partner's want.

It's also very important to pay attention to less obvious goals. In addition to what we're "after" in an argument, there are also goals that have to do with how we appear to others, and the relationships we maintain with them. Olivia did not throw a tantrum because she knew she was going to argue with Our Hero again, and did not want to poison the waters.

Sometimes the goals that are most important in a disagreement are not the obvious ones, but the goals that surround relationships. These goals, called *face goals*, are the goals we hold regarding how we want people to think about us, and how we want our relationships to be. A goal in one argument, for example, might be looking good in front of the boss. That might even mean abandoning the obvious argument goal and losing! Most of us have given in to a spouse or romantic partner even when convinced we are right. Why? Because the relationship goal is more important than the apparent goal. So we need to remember that goals are always manifold, always complex, and need to be watched for information and openings.

13. Zen and the Art of Argument

Many people are quick to tell me they are illogical, whatever that might mean; but very few people are truly illogical, and most of those are locked up. The people who claim to be illogical, usually with some barely hidden pride, are making a simple mistake: you can discover a conclusion any old way, but you can only convince someone else with reasons. Leaping to a conclusion does not make us illogical, just intuitive. When asked why you believe Harry is ruthless you will usually, if you keep at it, be able to tell. What you do is go back and follow the path of the intuition. If someone disagrees with the insight, then you are forced to defend it, give it up, or just go away. None of these is illogical.

> **Being illogical does not mean one is creative.**
>
> **Being illogical means one is crazy.**

So we are all, like it or not, logical. What we are doing here is getting better at it by learning the tricks and gambits used by those who would, consciously or not, manipulate us. At the beginning of this process many people are confounded by the quantity of new information. "How can I think of all this stuff and still argue?" The answer is the twofold path of argument.

The **first path** is that of knowledge. To increase your power and ability you must increase your knowledge of what can be done in arguments. That is the purpose of this book: to provide you with information in a way that it is natural and manageable. There is not a great deal to learn. Nothing I've explained so far should be new, it is just being made explicit. What was relied on unwittingly before is now conveniently laid out. In this fashion there is an opportunity to know what you are doing and what is being done to you. That is the purpose of these pages. You have a better idea of what to expect, where to go, and why you are going there. That knowledge will make your arguments more effective.

There is, however, this problem of keeping it all in mind, of thinking about it all when arguing. How is that possible? You cannot be listening *and* thinking about Principle Whatever at the same time; Super-Rule II does not permit it. The **second path** involves pushing all of this information away and just listening. It is like trying to remember someone's name. The harder you try, the more difficult it becomes. As soon as you give up and relax, as soon as you stop trying, the name comes to mind. This is how the twofold path works: the information is there, you have been accumulating it; by relaxing and listening you allow the mind to react freely to what is heard. A similar situation exists in sports. You can learn all there is to know about the correct tennis or golf swing, but thinking about the right arm while on the court or links is the worst thing to do. Instead, a coach will recommend you relax completely and clear your mind.

The Twofold Path of Argument

**The first path is learning
the tools and moves.**

**The second path is
concentration and relaxation.**

**One without the other does not
work.**

The references to Zen are only partially in jest. Like any other enterprise, argument may seem complicated and confusing. But its actual practice must be simple if it is to be effective: responses must take split seconds. Philosophers, in their daily activity, do not utter something and then wait ten minutes for a response. Nothing would be more boring. Instead, responses are fairly immediate, and as the temperature of the argument increases, so does the tempo of response. There is no great trick to learning to argue. It comes, like anything else, with practice. At first there is a need to refer more and more to the information; but this stage does not last long. Soon, even if you do not remember names and labels, you will be able to describe what your opposer is doing wrong. What does the name or label matter? Your opposer will not be impressed unless she too is familiar with the name. So the important information is contained in the moves and principles, not in their names.

The answer to the question "How do you think of all that stuff and argue at the same time?" is that you do not. Do not think about arguing, just listen, argue, listen, argue...

14. Section 1 Review

Questions

1. What are the most important parts of an argument?
2. Who can you trust in an argument?
3. How often do we argue?
4. How would you argue with someone who states, "I am against hanging for captial offences?"
5. Why is the Principle of Similar Cases so important to argumentation?
6. How often is Super-Rule II—*LISTEN!*—violated?
7. When *shouldn't* we argue?
8. Is **Super-Rule I** true?
9. What principle screams to be applied to this argument? "Of course the monarchy is a good thing, it's been around for 1000 years."
10. If my dispute partner and I are both getting a bit too emotional, what should I do?
11. What is the most important goal in an argument?
12. Do I have to argue, listen and think about the rules all at the same time to become a good arguer?

Answers

1. There are two basic parts to an argument. The first is the **claim** (or the conclusion) and it tells us what we are arguing about. The second are the **reasons** and they tell us why we are arguing about the claim. Make sure you have both before you commit yourself to a position.

2. **No one.** Someone who disagrees with you may intentionally or unintentionally use a fallacy or other misleading move. Someone who agrees with you may have completely different reasons and mislead your opposers.

3. **Very often.** Much of what we consider ordinary conversation is really argument. Anytime there is any disagreement—no matter how mild—the rules and procedures of argument come into play.

4. **You wouldn't.** Never argue against (or for) a conclusion without getting the reasons first. The speaker may be against hanging because he prefers boiling in oil!

5. The Principle of Similar Cases states that we will be consistent and will treat situations that are alike in the same way. Without such a rule we would never know what people were going to do, say or think. Being consistent requires arguers to bring all their beliefs and attitudes into alignment, and keeps them from being unreasonable.

6. Sorry, what was that you said?

7. There are two main times: first, when you do not know what you are talking about. In that case, just be quiet and try to get information. Secondly, when the person with whom you are arguing is much more emotionally involved than you are. In this situation be very careful, you can hurt someone badly without intending to.

8. **Of course not.** There are times, many times, when it is perfectly appropriate to say that you are wrong—just be sure, that's all.

9. **The Principle Principle.** The argument has within it the general rule, "things that have been around for 1000 years are worthwhile." Well, this would include quite a few items besides royalty such as cancer, poverty, and fascism.

10. Suggest you take a break. "It sounds to me like we're losing it. Let's take a short break, and then continue." Taking a break can be a major good thing to do in an argument.

11. It's impossible to say. The most important goal might be the apparent one – the topic of the discussion, or it might be a face goal. Only careful listening can tell.

12. No. You just have to listen carefully. One good way to practice is to listen to *both* sides of an argument when you are not involved.

Just sit back and pay attention to who is saying what to whom. Notice carefully who is listening, who is being irrelevant, and who is
committing fallacies.

Part   II

The Ways Of Argument

15. What's Going on Here?

Arguments are sometimes lost for a perfectly good reason: your opposer is right and you are wrong. But this, really, is the exception rather than the rule. Most arguments are not about subjects where right and wrong or true and false are clear. If an argument is about the weather, one person may be right and the other wrong. But if the argument concerns the opening of a new branch plant in Weehawken, a choice of summer camp for Jude, or the fairness of a Supreme Court decision, then there is no simple, correct answer. Usually the better argument will triumph. Since we are talking about arguments and not Truth a whole raft of items become relevant. How the case is presented, how well the position is known, how much thought has been given, how stubborn we are, the relationship between the opposers—all become factors affecting the outcome. An argument, for example, between two friends about baseball will have a very different character and feel from an argument between a boss and employee about proper business procedure.

In any argument there are moves which will make a case seem stronger than it is. They are traps. They appear to be innocent statements when in fact something has gone wrong. And it can be any one of a number of things. The subject of the argument might have been changed; alternative answers to the problem might have been sneakily limited; a source of information might have been unfairly dismissed. These are but three of a whole slew of maneuvers common to arguments. The traditional name for such mistakes is "fallacies." A fallacy is a trap that looks like a reasonable part of the argument but which actually conceals some unfair maneuver.

> **A fallacy may look good,
> but its beauty is a trap.**

Watch Our Hero fall for a classic fallacy.

OUR HERO: The whole question of capital punishment is very tricky.

JOSH: Tricky? How is it tricky?

OUR HERO: Well, for example, I was just reading an ad yesterday placed by the Association of Prison Guards. The ad pointed out that prisoners serving life terms cannot be punished any more severely.

JOSH: Well, what's so tricky?

OUR HERO: The guards are afraid that prisoners who are already serving life can kill prison guards and get off free. These prisoners have nothing to lose. That would scare me if I worked in a prison.

JOSH: Oh, sure. But look, the only reason they're concerned is because of their jobs. What else do you expect them to say? They're prison guards, so of course they're going to argue for capital punishment. Give me an argument from someone without such a vested interest and I'll listen.

OUR HERO: Well, I suppose they do have a vested interest, and no one else has given any good arguments that I've seen. I suppose you're right.

Josh has committed the fallacy of attacking the person. Instead of arguing about what the guards said he addressed their interest in the outcome. Sometimes this information might be relevant but it is not grounds for rejecting the argument. Our Hero has fallen for a very ancient trap.

What about Josh? Is he nasty? Underhanded? A cheat? Who knows? People who commit fallacies can do so by accident or on purpose. When Polly Politician does not answer a direct question it is probably intentional. Josh, on the other hand, may very well honestly believe that his reason for rejecting the guards' argument is a good one. All we can hope is that either Josh or Our Hero will read this book. Many fallacies are committed without any malice at all. When trapped in an argument people say whatever will get them out of trouble. So it's hard to fix blame in these cases.

> **Be careful—**
>
> **The nicest people can use
> the nastiest fallacies.**

Instead of worrying about who is guilty, we can learn how to handle these fallacies. Our Hero could easily have answered Josh by pointing out that the guards' argument might be offered by someone else without a vested interest, and then what would Josh say? So instead of laying blame we will concentrate on handling fallacies.

Each of the following sections discusses one or more fallacies. For each one several examples are given, and there are instructions for stopping the fallacy or getting around it. Finally, there are general strategy hints throughout, I urge you to search out fallacies in your daily newspaper and in conversations: like any other skill you must start out consciously practicing before the reactions and responses become automatic. So keep looking for examples of fallacies, and please send the best ones along to me. I collect them.

16. Ring Around the Argument

> MATTHEW: This book I just bought is great. I'm going to make a million because of it. It sure is a good buy!
>
> LAUREN: How do you know you'll make a million?
>
> MATTHEW: Well look, it says right here on page three that you'll make a million if you follow the instructions. I can't lose.

Matthew, as we all know, will not make a million through the advice in the book. The only ones who will certainly profit from the book are the author and publisher. What is more important, the argument Matthew gives Lauren is less than ideal. Here is another of the same ilk.

This guitar is very expensive and rare. It's handmade, and there are only two like it. If you don't believe me, ask the guy who sold it to me.

One more classic:

Of course we know that God exists. It says right in the Bible that God exists, and the Bible must be true since it's the word of God.

Whether or not Matthew makes a mint, the guitar is rare, or God exists, the arguments have something in common: *the reasons are only convincing if the claim is true*. But this is a fallacy since the truth of the claim is just what we are arguing about. If everything Mathew's book says is true, then he will make a million. But the book itself is hardly a place to look for reasons to believe it. It's like someone who says, "I'm really an honest guy. If you don't believe me, just ask me. I'll tell you the truth."

This fallacy is known by several names. The most familiar is "circular reasoning." Others are "begging the question" and the learned-sounding *petitio principii*. All allude to the central nature of the fallacy: the reasoning goes in a circle. One of the reasons is acceptable only if the conclusion is true, so the reason can hardly be used to support the conclusion. The argument presented above for the existence of God is not that far-fetched. I once had a discussion with a Hare Krishna devotee that went something like this:

> SCEPTIC: What makes you think that what this copy of the *Bhagavad-Gita* you are selling says is true?
> PEDDLER: My Guru says so, and he is a true guru.

Reasons are presented to support claims. Since you are arguing about the claim you need to have reasons for accepting or rejecting it. Sometimes one of the reasons means the same thing ("comes down to the same thing") as the claim. Since there is disagreement about the claim there must also be disagreement about any statement that means the same thing. So if you accept a reason that means the same thing as the claim, you have been tricked.

We argue *about* claims

by *examining* reasons.

Another example involves random testing. Often when a factory receives a shipment of something like ball-bearings they run tests to determine that the bearings are of high quality. Since they receive thousands of bearings at a time they cannot test them all. Instead they take out batches of ten at random and test perhaps ten batches of ten. In this way they can judge what the rest of the bearings are like. An engineer in charge of such an operation explained this to me once. This all makes a good deal of sense. But he went on: if, he explained, the first bearing of a batch of ten failed to pass the test, then that batch was thrown back in and another batch was chosen. The reason is that the highest failure rate expected is one in several thousand, so if the first bearing selected fails, the test will likely not accord with the expected results. In other words, the failure rate for this batch will be too high. This is blatantly circular, but not uncommon in statistics. It is circular since the testing by random choice is supposed to determine the failure rate. But instead of using the test to determine the failure rate, the expected failure rate is being used to determine the validity of the test. Everything has been turned upside down. And, oh, the engineer worked at a nuclear power plant.

> **An argument is *circular*
> or *begs the question* when
> one of the reasons
> assumes what it is supposed to
> prove.**

Another interesting example involves a discussion of changes to the welfare rules requiring people on welfare to work. One reason given by one commentator was that a just society does not penalize people for being poor. Why does that beg the question? Why is that circular? Well, how would anyone in favor of the changes react to the statement that a "just society" does not make people work for welfare? Surely someone arguing in favor of the changes must think they are just. So the justice of the rules and the society that creates them is what the argument is all about. Be very wary of evaluations such as "just," "good," "right," and so on in an argument. They frequently indicate a circular argument. They may occur with other reasons which are not circular, but they tend to bolster an argument in an unfair way. In the following example there are non-circular reasons as well as a circular one.

POLLY: You should vote for me next week. I am sincere, honest, and forthright. I support lower taxes and higher benefits. I am, what's more, the best candidate. So vote for Polly.

Forthrightness, honesty, and sincerity are valuable (though rare) traits in a politician, and provide, if true, reasons to vote for Polly. But what you are trying to determine in listening to speeches is who is the best candidate. Polly's announcing that she is the best begs the question: you want to know why she is the best.

The form of the fallacy is the same in relatively subtle cases like most of those above, or in more blatant cases like these two:

A.
OLIVIA: I think women should have equal rights.
JUDE: You think so, huh? Well I say it's crap.

B.
JUDE: The candidate says she'll lower taxes.
OLIVIA: That's nonsense and you know it.

In both examples the response begs the question. The simple assertion that a view is wrong is inadequate. Unless reasons are given for the rejecting the claim, the fallacy is committed. Sometimes reasons do follow the claim's dismissal, and then no fallacy occurs. So, if Olivia goes on, in B, to explain why she believes the candidate will not come through, she is not committing a fallacy. Usually, though, these summary rejections are not followed by reasons but left as is, in which case the fallacy is committed.

Another slightly different form involves labeling a view and then dismissing it because of the label. A common example finds an opposer throwing out accusations of "creeping socialism" or "more government subsidies" when that is exactly what is at issue.

> NATALIE: I think it's important that pregnant women receive special allowances for food.
> KELLY: That's just another instance of creeping socialism.

Indeed, perhaps it is. Natalie may not at all disagree. But we often fear and argue against the label rather than the issue. If Natalie goes on to maintain that it is not creeping socialism she may, in the end, convince Kelly. But Kelly may still be against the support—regardless of whether or not it is socialistic. Instead, Natalie should stay on track and not be misled into an argument about labels:

> NATALIE: Look, Kelly, call it what you want. I don't care if it's Socialism, Fascism, or Sufism, I think it's important because...

Now Kelly must deal with the reasons Natalie has given. Kelly's attempt at begging the question has been foiled.

**Reasons and points may hurt your position,
but names will never
harm you:**

*Don't fight about labels unless you
must.*

This same method can also be used in response to statements like "Nonsense," "Rubbish," and so on. Generally an arguer using a harsh response like that will feel fairly strongly about the issue. But you should respond to name-calling dismissals like "rubbish" in this way: "Perhaps. You may be right. But why do you think the view is rubbish?" A true question-beggar will respond with more non-reasons like, "I know rubbish when I see it." But stick to it. With perseverance you may force the name-caller to present an argument.

**Treat a dismissal like
"nonsense!"
as a claim and not as an argument.**

When the subtle form of circular reasoning occurs you can use a similar approach. The effect will be the same: you force the opposer to treat the fallacious reason like a conclusion. In this case a simple "Why?" will not suffice, but the strategy is simple: since the problem is that one of the reasons assumes too much, demand a justification for that reason. The conclusion cannot be offered as a justification for the reason, that would be too obvious a mistake. So a new reason must be brought in. You know, but your opposer may not, that you are really still arguing about the original conclusion; you just changed the wording.

**When the circularity is not blatant,
identify the circular reason
and demand
that it be justified.**

OUR HERO: It seems to me that the abortion laws ought to be loosened.

ZACK: By no means. That would be awful. How can you even think such a thing?

OUR HERO: Well, it seems to me that a lot of harm is being done to women who cannot get abortions.

ZACK: But how can you support murder? Every known society has rules and taboos against murder. Shall we be the only society that licenses murder?

Our Hero has to think fast. Zack's last comments are powerful and emotion-laden. How can he answer Zack's question? Who would want to approve of murder? Our Hero is not stuck—he knows what the problem is: Zack has begged the question—the argument is about the legitimacy of abortion. If abortion is legitimate it is not murder; if it is not legitimate it is murder—that is what the argument is about. Our Hero responds.

> OUR HERO: Frankly, Zack, it's not at all clear to me that abortion is murder. How can you be so sure?

The argument is still about the same thing, the rightness of abortion, but now the conclusion has changed from "abortion laws ought to be loosened" to "abortion is not murder." The important thing is that Our Hero knows what he is arguing about and so has been able to get round this circularity.

One last point. If the situation involves an audience Our Hero might choose a slightly different maneuver. Depending on how obvious the fallacy is, he might point it out. If it is blatant, or relatively blatant, an opposer can be made to look a bit foolish or sneaky. So Our Hero might have responded like this.

> OUR HERO: Good Lord. You can't call it murder. That's what we're arguing about! What are you trying to do?

This move applies to all fallacies, not just circular reasoning. We must be convinced that the audience will see it clearly. If not, we stand the risk of getting involved in a confusing explanation.

**Pointing out fallacies
can make opposer look
foolish or sneaky,
but be certain that your
audience will see it immediately.**

Begging the question is a common fallacy, but it can be beat. The surest way to beat it is to know your position. Red herring might be nice for breakfast, but in an argument it ends up tasting like crow.

17. What Were We Talking About?

One of the most common of all argumentative moves is one of the most infuriating. You're going along just fine, following and responding to your opposer's arguments, when all of a sudden you feel like you just walked into a strange conversation. Somehow there was a jump or switch which was missed, and you are overcome by a vague feeling of confusion. In many cases you find you no longer disagree, but your opposer is still arguing. When this occurs there has often been a change of subject. This move, the fallacy of changing the subject, is also called non sequitur, irrelevant reason, or, (ready?) *ignoratio elenchi*. Here I will call it "changing the subject," since that is the form that is most irritating and confusing. The following dialogue illustrates the fallacy.

> OUR HERO: I thought, Polly, that you were not going to support an increase in taxes if you were elected.
>
> POLLY: That's correct. I did not then anticipate such a need.
>
> OUR HERO: But yesterday you voted for an increase in school taxes. Why?
>
> POLLY: A politician must sometimes make unpopular decisions.
>
> OUR HERO: But why this one?
>
> POLLY: You wouldn't want me not to vote for taxes just so I might get re-elected, would you? Do you think an elected official should only do the popular thing?
>
> OUR HERO: No, of course not. But what I don't see is...
>
> POLLY: Well, this is one of those times when I had to put the good of our children above my personal ambitions. I'm sure we all agree that our children deserve the best of everything.

If Polly were at a press conference she would now smile and call for the next question.

Polly has eluded Our Hero by changing the subject. He asked her about a particular vote seemingly in violation of an election promise. Her answer was irrelevant: she wanted to vote that way. We already knew she voted that way, the question was "Why?" Notice how Polly presented her response in such a way as to elicit agreement. Yes, the taxes are unpopular, but are they worthwhile? Polly would be expecting agreement on the statement that a politician must follow her conscience, but would not be upset by disagreement, which would set the argument on a whole other course. We end up arguing on a subject Polly has chosen. Why should an opposer change the subject to something as dangerous as the original subject, namely the difference between her campaign promise and her vote? Surely, go to something safer. Here is another example.

> DIDI: Frankly, I think the schools should be closed. Children don't learn anything worthwhile there anyway.
> JOSH: I think you're being too extreme. They learn something. And it is the responsibility of society to see that children are educated. Surely you agree that it is our responsibility.
> DIDI: Of course we have that responsibility. But it's not being fulfilled by the schools.
> JOSH: Nonetheless, it is a very important responsibility and we should think very carefully of how we are going to fulfill it. After all, our children are our future. Aren't they the most vital aspect of our future?
> DIDI: Of course they are terribly important. That's why I want to close the schools.

Didi is giving Josh a run for his money. Josh wants to change the subject to the value of children, but Didi is keeping it on schools by quick agreement and repetition of the real subject. This way she can keep control of the argument. With any luck she will force Josh to deal with her position.

**When suddenly you no longer know
what you are arguing about,**

**check to see
if the subject was changed.**

The subjects which crop up as safe havens for harried opposers frequently include the wonders of children, the importance of the family, and, of course, patriotism. Here Michelle is ready to have a go with Josh:

> MICHELLE: It would be awful if the government gave all that money for helicopters right now. They probably will never be adequate, and we have far more pressing needs at this time.
>
> JOSH: But they are surely vital for defense. The Generals all say so.
>
> MICHELLE: Phooey. They are no more vital to defense than I am.
>
> JOSH: Everyone is vital to defense. Isn't this a democracy?
>
> MICHELLE: Of course, what's that got to do with it?
>
> JOSH: In a democracy everyone is vital to the nation. Everyone has an equal voice. Don't you think that's the way it should be?
>
> MICHELLE: In fact I do. But I don't believe everyone does have an equal voice, and you're naive to think so.

BOOM, and they are off and running. Josh has had better luck this time. Having safely left the topic (helicopters), he can freely agree with Michelle that it is a pity that not everyone has an equal voice. But he will never have defended his position on helicopters. Michelle committed a cardinal sin: she forgot what she was arguing about. She could have short-circuited Josh by not answering his question about democracy. She could have said something like, "It doesn't matter if this is a democracy or not, right now is a bad time to invest in expensive helicopters."

To avoid being caught by a change of subject, know what the argument is about and listen very carefully. If you are confused or unclear as to what your own position is, you can hardly accuse an opposer of changing the subject.

> **If you do not know what the topic is,**
> **you cannot expect**
> **your opposer to stay on it.**

So again, the best way to combat a particular fallacy is to know what you are doing. If you have a clear idea of what should be going on you will know the moment when your opposer leaves the track.

For a long time seat-belt legislation was a popular topic of debate. Should we be required by law to wear seat belts? Or is it a matter of personal choice? Do governments have a right to tell us what to do on this matter? In an argument I read once an opposer of seat-belt legislation attacked it on the ground that alcohol is the major cause of accidents. The defender of the legislation went on to argue this point. He was simply not quick enough to point out that the subject had been changed.

Every summer many sports magazines have a "swimsuit" issue. The issue is not dedicated to an analysis of what swim wear is best for racing or scuba diving, but rather it is an opportunity to increase sales by displaying a large number of scantily clad women. There have been protests made arguing that these displays have nothing to do with sports and are sexist and pornographic to boot. The publisher of one major magazine replied, "Our magazine is not porno. I've got an eight-year-old son and he looks at it." What is interesting about his answer is that it is probably true. But what does his son's reading habits have to do with the legitimacy of the contents of his magazine? Nothing at all.

Another non sequitur occurred in a letter to the editor complaining about Surgeon-General Koop's irritation at cigarette ads. The writer of a letter to the editor in the Toronto Star some years ago insists Koop not be taken seriously until he complains about beer ads. Perhaps the Surgeon-General should complain about beer ads, but what is the connection to cigarettes and their advertising? None.

The reporter interviewing the publisher, or Michelle, or Our Hero should obey Super-Rule II in this case. They should listen very carefully and notice the change in subject. For most arguers, constant obedience to Super-Rule II is too much to ask. Your mind wanders, and instead of listening to your opposer you think of your next statement or next question. All it takes is a moment's inattention to miss a switch. When it does happen, something unfortunate takes place: You get that feeling of bewilderment and you assume it is you, and not your opposer. In other words, when Our Hero gets confused he does not immediately say, "Where did that come from?" or "Why did you bring that up?" Instead he pretends he knows why the conversation has taken this turn and tries to hide his confusion by pretending he follows the argument. Familiar?

Most arguers do not have the confidence to suppose that the other person has made a mistake or committed a fallacy when it's so much easier to blame yourself: "There I go again, too stupid to know what's happening; too thick to follow the argument. Well, he's pretty bright, so I suppose he knows what he's talking about." Like hell. All you do with this attitude is compound a felony. First you forget to listen, then when you come back and are confused you assume it is you and not your opposer who is at fault. You can even do that when you are listening. Everything is going fine and then—POW!—confusion. Most arguers will assume they missed something their opposer said. But instead of saying, "Wait, I must have missed something," they pretend to understand every word and move. This is always bad. If the confusion is not caused by a mistake, then you owe it to our opposer to try to follow his argument. If the confusion is caused by a shifty maneuver, you owe it to yourself to stop and ask. In either case, whether the bewilderment is your fault or your opposer's, you should look for the cause.

Trust your instincts;
if you are confused there must be
a reason.

Check it out.

Another example will help illustrate why you have to stay on your toes. The following is an argument about the role of myth in history. Should history as taught to school children describe the truth? Or should the rough edges and nastiness—as, for example, cases of government corruption—be excluded or edited?

> OUR HERO: It's important that children grow up with a sense of reality. Teaching them that our country has never done wrong is a mistake. It gives them too strong a faith in leaders.
>
> EMMA: Well now, they're only children. You don't want to scare them.
>
> OUR HERO: It's not necessary to lay out every dirty fact. But presenting events as if there were no bad guys is too much. For one thing it's always contradicted by the daily newspapers. We're better off giving them the truth.
>
> EMMA: And what, pray tell, is that? Who knows what really happened in any situation? What is truth in history? You can never be sure that any description of an historical event is really complete.
>
> OUR HERO: [*Not falling for the bait.*] Sure, it's difficult to determine absolute truth in history or anywhere, for that matter. But that's not what we're talking about. There are obvious things left out, incidents not related, particularly when it comes to leaders doing shady deals. I'm not talking about absolute truth, that would be silly, as you, of course, know. What I am talking about is making the stories less like fairy tales.

This is a good example of pulling an opposer back to the subject. Our Hero sealed the return with the comment that Emma, *of course*, knows that absolute truth is not the issue. Now, instead of getting off on whether history can ever be the real truth, they are continuing with the discussion of myth in education.

Sometimes you may not want to be subtle about getting the subject back on track. It might be to your advantage to let an opposer know that you are aware of the subject change, that you know very well what is going on. You might be dealing with a constant subject-switcher, a real ground-changer. Most often these people, unless they are politicians, commit their fallacies unintentionally. Not only do they ignore your arguments and replies, but they do not even listen to their own. Since they have no idea what *they* are saying, it is nothing at all for them to say something else. So any time they are offered the least resistance they change the subject. Arguing with such people can be infuriating. In these cases the subject should be brought back firmly and obviously.

> # Be firm and obvious
> # with an habitual subject-switcher.

When you want to make a point of returning to the original subject first let your opposer finish. After your opposer has stopped, say something like, "That's fine. But we were talking about..., and I would like to continue." Or, "I'm sorry but you've changed the subject. I don't want to talk about that. Let's finish the first argument." A bit of time may have to be spent explaining why the subjects are different, but that is usually not too difficult. Watch Our Hero try this technique.

> OUR HERO: By no means should we re-institute a draft.
>
> OLIVIA: Well, I'm not so sure.
>
> OUR HERO: Having a large standing army is an invitation to use it. It creates hardship in a time when it is not necessary, and moves should be made to appear unwarlike.
>
> OLIVIA: But don't you think that people owe service to their country?
>
> OUR HERO: Look, Olivia, that's not what we're talking about. That's another story entirely. What I want to know is do you think a draft should be re-instituted?
>
> OLIVIA: Well, I just don't think there's anything wrong with serving your country.
>
> OUR HERO: Neither do I. But you're changing the subject. We're talking about one way of being forced to do it, not whether it's good or bad to ever serve your country in any way. Get back to the topic.

The difficulty is that some people never listen, and if they do not listen you cannot really argue with them. You might point that out, but results cannot be guaranteed. Everyone knows someone like good old Uncle Harry who hasn't heard a word anyone's said for years.

The key to beating a change of subject is first of all to know that it has happened. If the thread of an argument is lost, stop and find out what is going on. The chances are it had nothing to do with you.

18. Everyone's Doin' It, Doin' It, Doin' It

"Belcho Beer is the largest selling beer in the entire country. Could all those people be wrong?" This form of advertising is familiar to us all. What does it mean? How much weight does it carry? Take a look at one way in which Belcho's claim, while true, might be misleading. Suppose there was a beer industry composed of ten competitors, each with a fairly even share of the market: seven of them have exactly 10 percent of the total market, two have 9 percent, and one—you guessed it, Belcho—has 12 percent. So the difference which licenses Belcho's claim is 2 percent. Hardly that dramatic, though of course Belcho's stockholders are glad. But should *you* be impressed?

There is no fallacy committed when a company tells you that they are the leading product. The fallacy occurs if that is *all* they tell you. Why should you buy something just because everyone else is? It is interesting information, and it might even make you stop to consider the product, but it is not enough. "Most popular" does not always mean "best." There are always many reasons why a brand is the leading product, usually having to do with their marketing and advertising strategy. A good advertising campaign is much more important than quality. Other reasons contribute as well. Some products are very old and deeply embedded in the public mind. Other products are "first" because they have very few, sometimes poor, competitors. Any product can be "first" if it is the only competitor. Suppose you have a shampoo you want to advertise as the "leading" shampoo. Well, you cannot do that unless it is the leading shampoo. But wait. It may not be the *leading* shampoo, but it might be the *leading medicated* shampoo. And, if that is not enough, it might be the *leading medicated natural* shampoo.

> **Popularity alone
> is not enough.**

What is important is why something is popular. The fallacy of popularity occurs when popularity is taken as the most important fact. It has a fancier name which can be used to impress opponents: Argumentum ad populum, which means argument to the people. The factors contributing to popularity may be irrelevant in many cases. The very opposite view—that the most popular items will be disappointing—also makes sense. After all, for a product to sell very widely it must appeal to a very broad segment of the population. One way to do this is to make a very excellent product, but another way is to make a very bland product. So it should not be a surprise if Belcho Beer lacks character. Price is another factor important to popularity. Is the largest selling wine the best wine? What about the largest selling washing machine or dishwasher? Is it the best, or is there a more expensive one that will provide better service in the long run?

The fallacy of popularity has other forms as well. One of them is illustrated in the following dialogue.

> MATT: I really didn't expect the election to turn out that way.
> LAUREN: Well, it sure didn't fool me.
> MATT: How could you possibly have expected that? I though Smith was a shoo-in.
> LAUREN: Jones was an underdog. Everyone knows an underdog will wait and come from behind, just like Jones did. Anyone giving careful analysis would see that the underdog effect would work.

Lauren's last response to Matt involves two uses of the fallacy of popularity. The first uses the expression "everyone knows." Other familiar forms are "We all know", "It's common knowledge that ...," "You are, of course, aware, as we all are, that...," and so on. These are hard phrases to beat since everyone wants to be in the know. Since you do not want to appear ignorant or stupid, you agree to almost anything rather than admit ignorance. Lauren seals up the fallacy very tightly the second time: "Anyone giving careful analysis..." This expression has close relatives in "Anyone giving a moment's thought," or "Anyone who knows what's happening," and so on. To disagree with Lauren is like saying, "I did not give a careful analysis." Watch:

> OUR HERO: Choosing a car is difficult. It looks to me like a Ford is somewhat better made than a Chevy.
> DIDI: Nonsense. Anyone who knows their cars would tell you that a Chevrolet is better than a Ford.
> OUR HERO: Well, I guess I don't know cars because I just don't see it that way. Why does everyone think Chevrolet is better?

Didi is now on the spot, and must put up or shut up. If she thinks everyone knows, then *she* must know, so the Principle of Rationality insists she have reasons. If not she will look foolish and lose her credibility as well.

If your opposer says that everyone knows...
and you don't know,

then what she said was wrong.

We are our own evidence. Everyone, according to our learned opposer, knows that Smith is in the pocket of big business. But if *you* do not know that, if *you* do not have good reasons for believing it, then *you* have disproved your opposer's claim: you, after all, are part of everyone.

It is difficult to respond to the popularity fallacy in the correct way. Remembering one thing might help: not only is it a fallacy, but your opposer's statements are very often just false. Rarely does everyone know something terribly interesting. Very few people do the necessary work to find out, so they are just repeating what some opposer told *them* that everyone knows. This is called rumor, not fact; a rumor is something that should be checked, not believed. This fallacy does not depend on your ignorance for its success, but on your fear of *seeming* ignorant. Not attacking the fallacy lets your opposer know that you are not only ignorant but gullible, so you are better off attacking.

Never let the fear of looking dumb make you argue poorly.

You're no dumber than anyone else.

Sometimes the appeal is not to something everyone knows, but it is still a fallacy. An example involves the mistake called "provincialism," or assuming that what is close and familiar is better. When, for example, you know something such as a city or country it is very easy to assume that *your* city or country is better than any other. Such assumptions usually are false. It is just nice to think that our country or religion or lifestyle is best: it feels good to believe that you are superior or are free from errors and faults that other people have. This often leads to a belief that our country can do no wrong, or that our religion is the only real one. One way to reinforce this is in education: teach children that their country has never done wrong, or that their religion is better than all the others. When, in later life, they are faced with a foreign religion, a strange life-style, or the possibility that their country has committed some underhanded or immoral act they will be totally unprepared to deal with it. It is much easier to believe what we know and like than what is strange and different.

A similar situation is common in race relations: *My* race is tolerant, under-standing, kind, and generous. *They*, on the other hand, are pushy, intolerant, nasty, and selfish. The psychological foundations of prejudice are complicated and not at all clear, but the role of prejudice in argument is simple: believe whatever supports your own group. This fallacy extends far beyond argument to a whole way of perceiving the world: many people refuse to listen to or hear those things that threaten the foundation of their beliefs. One of these threats comes from a demand for equality from other races and nations. If you have reasons for not agreeing, fine and well, but it is your responsibility to acknowl-edge those reasons and to let them be known. The beauty of argument is that is knows no favorites. The same rules apply to all the participants.

19. Well, If He Said So...

It is impossible to know everything. No matter how much you read and discuss, you cannot become expert in every field. Once plumbing is conquered, biology remains. If theoretical physics is under control, then auto mechanics is baffling. There are just too many areas of expertise.

Normally this is not a hardship because no one wants to know everything. But there are times when information not known to you is important when having an argument or making a decision. In these situations you generally call on an expert. The expert may not be a famous scientist or movie star, but simply the local auto mechanic, or your family doctor. Sometimes the expert might be a friend who is "in the business" or an acquaintance who knows something or someone.

Suppose you are thinking about buying a new stereo system. You might well talk to salespeople or friends who are enthusiasts. For your purposes in this discussion, each of these people can be considered an expert.

> **An expert is anyone
> who knows more than we do when
> we want to know it.**

So your neighbor with the $6500 stereo who reads four media magazines a month and talks freely about tweeters, woofers, and wattage is an expert, as is the audio engineer married to cousin Kathy.

The problem in dealing with experts is the very reason for dealing with them: they know more than you do. It is all too easy to be misled by an expert. The neighbor with the $6500 setup may be of very little help if you are planning to spend a total of only $800. Yet expert advice is essential: It would be foolish to spend $800 on hi-fi equipment without seeking information from those who know.

Often the situations requiring experts are both complicated and controversial. A great deal of the debate on the safety of video display terminals, for example, involves conflicting expert testimony. In recent times, more than ever before, the expert is being challenged both by other experts and by the public. The popularity of issues such as environmental control, space exploration, and even corporate expansion and monopoly have led to pitched battles—in public—between experts on all sides.

The difficulties posed by the need for experts are easily overcome. The first and most vital step is the elimination of awe. For some reason perfectly capable, intelligent people lose all perspective when dealing with someone who knows something they do not.

> **Remember—**
> **you are an expert, too,**
>
> **and you know how little you know.**

Virtually every one of us is capable of giving reasonable advice on some subject or other. It may have to do with your job, or it may involve a hobby or pastime, but there is surely at least one small area on which you might be asked for and offer advice. So each of us, in that area, is an expert. At the same time you know perfectly well that the advice given will be subject to prejudices, training, needs, and experience. Suppose, for example, that Jacob is a hi-fi buff. He may well be asked by a friend for advice on purchasing some equipment. But just because he is familiar with the field he is also aware of the complications. Jacob knows, for example, that his friend should spend his money one way if he generally listens to classical music and another way if he is a rock fan. This is obvious. But when you want advice from someone else, all this is forgotten. Too often anything they say will be taken as the gospel truth—after all, they know what they are talking about. If you apply the same caution to other experts that you apply to yourself you'd be off to a good start.

One of the most frequent mistakes involving experts occurs when they are used in the wrong field. The most obvious example of this sort of fallacy is the performer who recommends a product. Ray Charles might very well be worth listening to on the merits of musical instruments, and I would not at all mind his advice on buying stereo equipment, but is he an expert on soft drinks? I have seen a photograph of a Dallas Cowboy quarterback attached to promotional material for heavy tractors. There is no indication at all that even the best quarterback is prepared to choose intelligently among heavy tractors.

> **No one is simply an expert—**
> **an expert must be**
> **an expert**
> ***in something.***

The expert you are seeking out or the one being used against you by an opposer in an argument must be from the right field. The examples involving athletes selling cars and tractors are the most blatant, but others are harder to identify. A famous example involved Doctor Benjamin Spock during the height of the anti-Vietnam war movement. The doctor, an expert in child care, was all of a sudden taken to be an expert on foreign affairs. There is, of course, absolutely no reason why Dr. Spock should not have spoken out as he did. He had every right to do so, indeed he claimed that he had an obligation to do so. But what was wrong was that Spock's fame or achievements as a pediatrician somehow lent greater authority or force to his opinions. Spock's arguments should have stood or fallen on their own merits, and not on his reputation as a pediatrician.

In recent years it has seemed almost impossible to get elected without an entire supporting cast right from Hollywood. We should not care who Jane Fonda, Madonna, Tom Cruise, or any other star is voting for—and that is absolutely no reflection on them, their intelligence, or their talent. They are just not experts, and if they are treated as such then the fallacy of appeal to authority, or argumentum ad vericundiam, is committed.

> **If the expert appealed to**
> **is not appropriate,**
>
> **then a fallacy is committed.**

One of the real difficulties with experts is that it is very hard to identify just what they are expert in. If you are arguing with a biologist, you should not expect him to know everything about every branch of biology. A good auto mechanic, after all, should refer you to a specialist when it comes to problems with your transmission.

So how careful do you have to be? The answer depends on how technical and narrow is the information you want. If it is a general question in biology there is no need to get a specialist. But if the argument is about a very fine point, perhaps the effect of a chemical on a fish or animal, then a high degree of specialization is required. The way to determine if the expert is the specialist is to ask. The following dialogue illustrates this. Notice how Our hero diminishes the standing of the authority.

> JUDE: Yes, that substance in the water should not have the effect on the adrenal gland that Professor Martin describes.
>
> OUR HERO: Is endocrinology the field in which you do your work?
>
> JUDE: No, not exactly. I'm in a closely related field.
>
> OUR HERO: Have you ever written anything or lectured on endocrinology?
>
> JUDE: No. But it forms a part of the regular program of study for any biologist.
>
> OUR HERO: I see, So really you don't know any more about it than any other biologist. Professor Martin, on the other hand, is an endocrinologist, isn't he?

The authority has been put in his place: he is not a specialist in the field. All too often we are impressed by scientists because they are scientists, not because they know what they are talking about.

Authorities can appear very impressive even when their colleagues might not be moved. An expert with a Ph.D. in economics, a list of credentials, and a great private fortune might recommend investing heavily in the commodity market when most other financial advisers would not. You may not know if you are being given an unusual opinion or a standard response. Assuming that other authorities would agree with this expert might be a mistake.

**Is the authority giving you
generally accepted facts
or an unusual personal opinion?**

Find out.

Here is how this problem might be handled.

> OUR HERO: I don't know. The commodities market is supposed to be very tricky and dangerous. Are you sure about this recommendation?

LORYN: Certainly. That is the very best place, right now, to make money.

OUR HERO: I'm really surprised. Would most financial consultants agree with this advice?

LORYN: The smart ones would.

OUR HERO: But would most of them?

LORYN: No, most wouldn't. They try to scare people out of the commodities market for no good reason.

Our Hero should be satisfied that the expert is a maverick offering a controversial opinion rather than mainstream advice. This does not mean the expert is wrong, just that caution should be used. After all, the whole problem in consulting authorities is that you have to accept their word for something. And if their word is not generally agreed upon, the value of their advice is diminished.

Other ways of checking out the experts include examining their track records and investigating what other beliefs they hold. These areas should especially be checked when using an expert publicly. You can be embarrassed when offering an expert's agreement if your opposer replies, "Oh, yes. I've heard of him. He's the guy who thinks cats and dogs should be made to wear diapers in public." Even if your man is the very best in the field, his credibility has been undermined. Another danger is that the authority may be in the habit of making rash predictions. The expert may have a bad case of news-conference-itis, a disease sometimes plaguing the scientific establishment. Not quite as embarrassing as the first example, it will still not help the cause if the expert is remembered as having predicted that the ozone layer would completely vanish by 1993.

Know your experts:

Do they hold embarrassing beliefs?
Do they make rash predictions?

We must all at times deal with experts, from those who profess to understand complicated issues and burning questions on down to your neighborhood auto mechanic and family doctor. Dealing with these local experts is a chilling experience for many people. Computer experts often seem to revel in the combination of their special knowledge and our ignorance. As your technical information on computers increases through valiant attempts to learn from books and manuals, so do the machines themselves change and become more and more complicated. Many males, bearing the cross of "being supposed to know," have purchased manuals entitled "Understanding Your Computer: A Guide for Women," or one of those books designed for the technologically impaired. The computer saelsperson knows you are reluctant to admit ignorance. There is nothing worse to some males than having to admit ignorance about machines. This is, sadly, becoming common among females as well: knowledge about the computer is now one among many symbols of competence. But the problem is still there—most of us are abysmally ignorant about the stupid machines.

There is a solution to the difficulties of dealing with computer consultants, and it applies to auto mechanics, plumbers, plasterers, doctors, and others. The requirement for using the solution is stiff: you must actually feel pride in your ignorance. After all, you might be an accountant, or stock clerk, or homemaker, or whatever; and it is just not part of your job to know about RAM or megabytes, so why should you? The very reason for going to an expert is because it is her job. So the first half of the solution is to freely admit, even flaunt, your ignorance. This prevents premature agreement.

> **Never agree with an expert**
> **unless you really do know**
> **what she is talking about, —**
>
> **no matter how stupid you feel.**

A real expert is very familiar with her work. She is so familiar that she should be able to explain it to anybody, even if you are completely ignorant about the subject. You must demand explanations from local experts until you really do understand. They may not like it. I am convinced the service manager of my local auto dealership has homicidal fantasies about me, but I cannot tolerate the thought of paying all that money without knowing why. So my answer is to doggedly persist in questions until I really do understand what is going on. There is a temptation to say, "Oh, sure. If the frammis is frozen you have got to replace the geegaw." But why pretend when I don't even know a frammis from a geegaw?

Remember what I pointed out at the beginning of this chapter: you are an expert. It is only reasonable that there are things you do not know. It is also reasonable (and this is truly liberating) that there are things you do not want to know. So remember, in dealing with an expert, ignorance can be your most important weapon. The key to dealing with experts is to demand an explanation: an expert should be able to explain to anyone. Any expert doing less should be viewed with suspicion. Any expert refusing to explain her decision is violating the Principle of Rationality and should be avoided.

20. The Refuge of Scoundrels

Arguing can be a long, tiring, involved business. Getting someone to agree, attempting to change someone's mind, can take a good deal of effort. Simple persuasion, on the other hand, when there is no concern for method, truth, honesty, or principle is another matter. When argument is forsaken in favor of manipulation, considerable time and effort can be saved. Often people who are very sure of the truth of their position, (or the justness of their cause or the importance of their goal,) will care only about results. In these cases a frequently used device is the "attack on the person."

Polly politician is running for office again and is quite insecure about this election. She knows she is the better candidate and so has a right to use whatever means necessary to defeat her foe. Here is a part of her speech to an audience of veterans. Counting on the fact that she's addressing a generally conservative group and is receiving newspaper attention, she freely smears her opponent:

> POLLY: I am running for office; not for myself; not for glory; not for my party. I will accept great burdens for my self and my family in taking this job. Why then shall I do it? I do it for one reason only: my country. [Applause.] Does my country need me? Of course not, Whom am I? Just a citizen and voter like you. I am just someone with a deep devotion to this great land and the principles on which it stands. Why then do I run? The answer is simple: there are those who would undo all the great things, all the great principles, fought for by all the great patriots who have lived and died for this country throughout its glorious history. [Applause.] I speak of those who are not devoted to the family, to freedom, but who are self-serving and confused. I speak of those who would lead us in their confusion into the hands of the devil, of our enemies. Is my opponent a womanizer? A devil worshipper? A pederast? I do not know. But I don't care about labels. Just look at his policies: where do his sympathies lie? I ask you, who can you trust?

Polly can go on indefinitely. She has not directly called her opponent a per-
vert, but simply created a strong association. She is name-calling. She has not
dealt at all with her opponent's statements, issues, or policies. This is a very
powerful device before a sympathetic audience. This nasty and underhanded
form of attack to the person was used by Senator Joseph McCarthy during the
witch hunts of the fifties. It really is very simple: it is almost impossible to prove
that you are not something. Imagine that someone has accused Liz of being dis-
honest and sneaky. How would Liz go about proving that person wrong? It is
impossible. She may call witnesses from among friends, relatives, and acquain-
tances, but they are all dismissed since they all like her and can hardly be expected to say anything else. The only other thing Liz might do is point up times
when she did particularly honest things. But this is all just evidence showing
how sneaky she is: real sneaks are never discovered; they always appear to be
honest and trustworthy. This sort of smear tactic, also called an argumentum ad
hominem, is hard to beat.

There are a number of different attitudes concerning the correct response to
this sort of attack. One is to ignore it. But are such smears ever really ignored?
Another response is to say it does not deserve the dignity of a reply. But in doing so one has replied, saying implicitly that the charge is nonsense. A good
reply might be, "These tactics are used from time to time in every campaign.
Some people will stoop to anything, and I think that is the most interesting point
to arise from Polly's statements. I leave it to the voters to decide if they want me
or someone who uses smear tactics and name-calling." This is still traditionally
labeled "refusing to reply."

Another possible response makes use of humor: "Sure, I know that Polly
called me a leftwinger. She'd probably label Lincoln a leftwinger for freeing the
slaves. She's so far to the right she has to look backwards just to make a left
turn." But all these situations fail if the context is not public. Someone accused
at work, for example, will likely never get a chance to reply in any way at all. So
that best reaction all around is to point up the evil as it is happening. "What is
your evidence for saying Liz is a sneak and a gossip? Come on, what gives?" By
reacting in this way you have a reasonable hope that you will be saved when it is
your turn.

> **If someone attacks
> a person's character,
> insist that he put up or shut up.**

There are other forms of name-calling which are very common but not quite
as out-and-out vicious. Here the opposer describes those who disagree in an unfavorable way. Usually they are dismissed as "naysayers" or "dissidents" or "a

small minority of unsatisfied diehards." What these phrases mean is that the individuals disagree, which is perfectly accurate. The implication, however, is that nothing would satisfy these people. One of the most famous of all such labels harks back to the much-quoted dismissal of anti-Vietnam war protesters used by Spiro Agnew, vice-president under Richard Nixon. He labeled those who disagreed with the war effort, "an effete corps of impudent snobs." Nowadays they are more likely to be referred to as "thoise who refuse to stay the course," but it's still name-calling Let us watch Our Hero in a brief interchange with Polly:

> OUR HERO: Tell me, Polly, what is your opinion of the charges leveled against the proposed atomic energy plant?
>
> POLLY: Atomic energy is a cheap, safe, sure source of fuel.
>
> OUR HERO: That's nice, Polly. But tell me about your reactions to the criticisms.
>
> POLLY: These people are nothing but a small group of fanatics trying to undermine a vast, important project that will benefit many people and create 129 new jobs.
>
> OUR HERO: O.K. Just tell me one thing: Are the fanatics right?
>
> POLLY: Of course not. They are just know-nothing do-gooders.
>
> OUR HERO: But *why* are they wrong, Polly?
>
> POLLY: You'll have to excuse me, but I have another appointment across town.

Imagine Polly at home one night. Surely her reply to a question from her husband about her plans for the evening would be something like this: "Indeed, the evening is a most important part of the day and plans should definitely be considered." Our Hero realized that the question is not how the dissidents are to be labeled, but how we respond to their arguments. Even when the nasty names really apply to people, their arguments stand or fall on their own worth, not the worth of whoever offered the argument. According to newspaper reports a politician recently labeled two constituents as "ding-dongs" because they'd written him letters opposing a pay raise for legislators. An effective reply would be, "I have been called a ding-dong. Well and fine. But what this ding-dong wants to know is how can these pay raises be justified."

> **Labels apply to people,**
> **not**
> **their arguments.**

Another sort of attack addressing itself to the person and not the argument aims to discredit someone because of who they are, because of their circumstances. Dismissing an argument by prison guards just because they are prison guards constitutes a fallacy: it is just not a good enough reason. During the Pinochet dictatorship in Chile, the Chilean Ambassador to Canada responded to charges of torture there by calling those who gave testimony on the subject "political enemies of the Chilean government who have long been absent from the country." This attack is irrelevant since it is about their background and not their statements. I have seen similar claims made by Iranian and South African ambassadors as well.

These days an especially insidious form of argumentum ad hominem stalks the land. People are accused of not being against terrorism because they disagree with a government position. Opposing a law or a position that is intended to fight terrorists does not mean that you support terrorism. It means you are not satisfied with the way in which it is being fought. Attacking an opposer because they disagree with you rather than attacking the reasons presented is an example of the fallacy.

> **Disagreeing with**
> **a position or a law,**
> **does not mean**
> **you are against its intent.**

Personal circumstances are usually irrelevant to the truth or falsity of a claim. An interviewer was once questioning the Reverend Jesse Jackson about the busing issue. At one point a whole series of questions was raised about Jackson's lifestyle. Jackson was asked where he lived, the size of his car, the size of his house, and so on. Jackson might live in a mansion or a one-room shack—it matters not at all to his argument. It might matter for other things, but not for determining the value of his argument about school busing. Jackson unfortunately, went on to address himself to these points rather than simply point out their irrelevance.

Our Hero will have a crack at dealing with an attack to the person:

> OUR HERO: Probably the stickiest argument against abortion is the one about the sanctity of life. I don't know how to dismiss that one at all.
> ANNE-LISE: Oh, you mean the Catholic argument.
> OUR HERO: Yes, that one.
> ANNE-LISE: Well, only Catholics hold that position, and they're *all* against abortion.
> OUR HERO: So?
> ANNE-LISE: Well come on, the only reason they put forward an argument like that is because they're against abortion in the first place. If they weren't against abortion they would never say that.
> OUR HERO: Sure, Anne-lise, but it's still an argument. I have no idea, really, whether anyone believes it—but that just doesn't matter. What we need is a counter-argument.

Our Hero has stopped Anne-lise from dismissing the argument simply because it is presented by Catholics. They may well be pushing the position because they are Catholics: Anne-lise may be right. But it is still necessary to eliminate the argument, rather than the person or the group.

The most common way in which this fallacy occurs is through the use of an expression like, "Well, what would you expect her to say? After all, she's..." followed by the explanation of his interest in the case. A train conductor arguing for improvements in rail service, a general arguing for more defense funds, an ecologist warning about future shortages, a professor extolling the virtues of higher education—to all of these it is easy to reply with a dismissal since you "know what they think." And it might even be true that the arguments these people give is exactly what you would expect them to say. But so what? Now that they have said it, what will you reply?

> **A person's background may ex-**
> **plain**
> ***why* they give an argument,**
> **but it will not be**
> **grounds for dismissing it.**

One difficulty with the attack to the person is that in some situations a person's background and character are important. For example, when someone is presented as an authority certain aspects of his or her background become relevant. So an authority's track record, history, and standing within a particular community of experts may be relevant in determining his or her reliability. And, speaking of testimony, information about a person's character and background may be relevant in a court of law. If someone giving testimony has a reputation as a liar or perjurer, you can be sure that a lawyer will want the jury to know about this witness's history. There is, though, an obvious difficulty captured in the story of the boy who cried wolf: someone may well have a reputation for lying and yet be telling the truth in this instance. For this reason it is imperative that character assassination or even character investigation be limited to those times when it is absolutely essential.

The traditional name of the fallacy of attacking the person is the argumentum ad hominem. It is the fallacy most commonly known by its Latin tag, and you may have heard people dispute a claim by saying something like, "That's no good. It is just an ad hominem." The error is a form of an even more general move, traditionally called the genetic fallacy, which involves confusing the truth or falsity of an argument with its origins.

The genetic fallacy occurs when governments buy from certain firms for reasons other than the value of the product. If, for example, geographic location or economic factors are considered, then, if the reasons for using this information are not given and defended, the genetic fallacy is committed. Another traditional situation involves the origin of ideas. An idea or invention might be rejected (or accepted) just because it is Russian or Chinese or Islamic. Watch:

> OUR HERO: Wouldn't it be great if all the government officials and bureaucrats had to spend time at physical jobs, and maybe even be required to go to government offices *incognito* to get forms or information? I think that would really make them nicer, more responsive to our problems.
>
> JOSH: Oh, no you don't. I know where that comes from. That's the sort of nonsense that went on in China, isn't it?
>
> OUR HERO: Yes. They had whole systems geared to keeping officials in touch with the problems of the ordinary people.
>
> JOSH: Foo. I don't go for any of that commie stuff here. We have enough problems of our own without starting that sort of nonsense.

The best thing for Our Hero to do now is quit the argument. He might lie and say they are trying it out in England, but I hope that is beneath him.

**When an argument is attacked
for its source or its origins
the fallacy of
ad hominem
has been comitted.**

A last common form of this fallacy is the dismissal of ideas that have previously gotten into trouble. Like children caught in the act, they are condemned to a future marked with doubt and mistrust. Socialized medicine or guaranteed income or whatever, may have flopped somewhere, but unless reasons are given for supposing it will not work here a fallacy has been committed. There are so many things that can go wrong you just cannot know that an idea will not work if tried in a different place and in a different manner. Bottle and can recycling programs may thrive in one area and flop miserably in another. The failures provide opportunities to learn for the next attempt; they do not necessarily mean the idea itself is wrong.

Name-calling, smearing, and dismissing arguments because of their source are all ways of avoiding the real issue. These tactics are common among those who do not wish to listen or consider. So beware: if a person's character, motives, or background is raised, demand to know why it is relevant to the argument.

21. The Straw-Man Argument

Shadow-boxing can provide a person with exercise, training, and a feeling of accomplishment. But there is a catch: When finished with the boxing drill one cannot turn around and say, "Well, I sure beat him." After all, no one was beaten; it was all make believe. There is a similar situation in argument. Sometimes an arguer will viciously, mercilessly, and dramatically destroy a position. The destruction is total and the position is in ruins. But, the arguer was shadow-arguing: no one holds the attacked position. The arguer was fighting an imaginary foe not just in the sense that no opposer was present, but also in the sense that no opposer could be found.

It frequently happens in arguments that a position is attacked when there is really no one there to defend it. Here is a quick vignette illustrating this situation:

> LAUREN: What do you think of this teachers' strike?
> MATT: I think they want to run the whole school system all by themselves, and that, as far as I am concerned, is crazy.
> LAUREN: What do you mean?
> MATT: There should be community involvement as well as teacher input. And there is no way the whole board of education should be thrown out just because teachers say so.
> LAUREN: Well, I certainly wouldn't want to chuck out the board.

Lauren is now agreeing with Matt. They are agreeing on Matt's version of the striking teachers' demands. It would be interesting to see if they would agree on the real demands. Did Matt really capture the sense of the demands? Do the teachers really want all decision-making power? Do they not want any other group, particularly the board or parents, to have a say? These are very radical, strong desires. In fact, they are suspiciously strong. Are there really any teachers who hold this view? And if so, are they a large enough group for their views to be labeled "the teachers' view"? There may be *some* teachers who hold the position described by Matt, but how many?

The *fallacy of the straw man* is committed when a position is distorted. The position is made more radical or extreme than it really is, making it easier to attack. A student might have several interesting arguments for the abolition of grades in a university. Rather than dealing with these arguments, an opposer might portray the student's position as one that calls for eliminating any evaluation and giving out degrees just for the asking. This is a much easier position to attack. Another example involves abortion debates. By characterizing the opposition as far more radical than it is, an opponent of abortion is able to point out many awful results following liberalization. If the opposition describes the position as not having a time limit after which abortions may not be performed, the pictures and verbal descriptions of late-term abortions will provide endless hours of emotional ammunition. If the position were more accurately portrayed, this would not happen.

> **When given a radical position,**
> **ask yourself:**
>
> **Does anyone really hold this view?**

Not all instances of the straw-man fallacy are intentional. Sometimes people really do misunderstand a position, or they may have been given wrong information. Nonetheless, the distortion is still there. What complicates matters even more is that the media, for instance, always give more play to the most radical fringe of any group.

> **Given any position,**
> **no matter how crazy or extreme,**
> **you can always**
> **find someone who holds it.**

People on the radical fringe, just because they are so outrageous, make for more interesting listening and reading than the moderate members of a group. Consequently, it is the radical fringe we hear about. A well-known example is the women's rights movement back in the early seventies. The vast majority of women were essentially moderate, but the media reported almost exclusively on those elements of the movement that were sure to get the strongest reaction.

In the following dialogue Our Hero will smell a rat and try to get more information.

> JOSH: You know, I think these environmental groups are crazy.
>
> OUR HERO: Why crazy?
>
> JOSH: Well, if they had their way we'd shut down every factory, boom, just like that.
>
> OUR HERO: Really?
>
> JOSH: Really. And the economy would come to a grinding halt—massive unemployment, enormous dislocation, starvation and anarchy. Just to save some trees.
>
> OUR HERO: Well, that certainly does seem like a high cost to pay. Are you sure that's the position.
>
> JOSH: You bet it is. But they're fanatics, so what can you expect.
>
> OUR HERO: Well, Josh, maybe some extremists would hold that position, but I can't believe many do. There must be a lot in favour of cleaning up factories instead of closing them. Maybe we should do some research.

Our Hero was alerted by the following rule of thumb:

> **Always be very suspicious of positions that are too easy to attack:**
>
> **They have very likely been distorted.**

Distortion of our view can be eliminated by interrupting with something like this: "That's a very interesting view. However, it has nothing to do with my position. Let me explain again." In the next dialogue Osh will try to saddle Our Hero with a radical position:

> OUR HERO: There is too much money spent on defense in this country.
>
> OSH: I suppose what we ought to do is just invite our enemies in for a picnic. Is that what you think?

HOUR HERO: Don't be silly. I'm not against defense,
I'm just questioning the amount.

OSH: If we don't have a strong defense force we'll be
overrun. Would you want that?

OUR HERO: Look, Osh, I don't know what you're getting so excited about. I don't want to eliminate the defense
budget or throw out our defenses. All I'm suggesting is that
too much is being spent. There probably is an incredible
amount of waste.

OSH: Too many people these days find it easy to attack
things they don't know anything about. Defense is vital to survival. When you cut defense spending you're cutting down
our chances of survival. I think that's dangerous, unless you
don't want us to survive.

OUR HERO: What nonsense, Osh. You're distorting everything. Who said anything about not surviving? Don't put
your words in my mouth.

Josh seems to be fairly uninterested in Our Hero's argument. All he is trying to do is scare Our Hero. This is a common form of distortion: altering the
position into one which is immensely unpopular or dangerous. If you are not
careful you can succumb to the fear and abandon the position. This is a form of
browbeating not uncommon in situations where loyalty or patriotism may seem
to be an issue. In most cases it is only the distortion that makes patriotism relevant.

The only proof against distortion is observance of Super-Rule II. If you are
always listening you will hear any distortions and object to them. Please remember that you must listen to *your own arguments* as well as to our opposer's.
In this way you will be aware of any differences between your version and your
opposer's. The ability to know your position is crucial: you cannot reasonably
expect to win arguments if you are defending distortions.

22. The Slippery Slope

Way back in the very first chapter of Part I Our Hero encountered an unco-operative civil servant. The clerk feared that if he reached over for the form Our Hero wanted, in no time at all he would be running about all over the place fetching this and that for everyone. The clerk would have to run to the insurance department in the next room to get insurance forms, to the certification office upstairs to get certification forms, and on and on endlessly. And the clerk is quite right in not wanting to carry this burden. After all, he is paid a modest wage for standing behind a window and giving out one sort of form. Yet his argument contained a fallacy: he need not go to any of those other places at all; he need not move off his seat at all; all he need do is reach over for the requested form. The clerk's argument was that if he fulfilled Our Hero's request, he would then have to perform those other duties. This is where the fallacy lies. The same reasons do not apply to getting a form upstairs as apply to his reaching over to the next window. As soon as the situation changes, the reasons change. The Principle of Similar Cases states that situations treated differently must be different, and there is a considerable difference in time, energy, and impact on those waiting if the clerk goes away from his post. So there is no good reason to accept his argument—as the situation changes, so will the reasons.

> **You will slide down the slippery slope
> unless you remember**
>
> **that different statements
> need different reasons.**

The clerk viewed the situation as if he were on top of a steep slippery slope: if he takes just one step onto the slope he will slide down and not be able to stop himself. Most situations are not at all like slippery slopes, but more like staircases: At each step you can stop and decide if you should go on by examining the next step down. Sometimes the distance between two steps is so small that we fail to see the difference. For example, this occurs often to people when they are purchasing a new car. The salesman, making a pitch for the options, will frequently point out that you have already decided to spend $15,500 and all he is talking about is $1000 for air conditioning. After all, if you are already spending such a large sum how much more will the small amount increase it? This is fine except that you do have to pay the $1000, and more if you keep up this sort of reasoning.

Sometimes slopes really are slippery, and it becomes impossible to draw a line between two steps on the slope. This occurs in the arguments concerning abortion because it is important to know when a fetus becomes a person. Simply put, if a fetus is a person it has rights, and in particular the right not to be killed. Witness part of a debate on abortion between Our Hero and Sophie:

> DIDI: I don't see what the fuss is about. Sure a baby just before it's born is a person, but not at, say, six weeks. How can you compare the two?
>
> OUR HERO: Well, they certainly are different. But let me ask you this: you say that just before birth, let's say at eight months, a fetus is a person.
>
> DIDI: That's right. I confess that the few moments before birth can't make the difference between a person and a non-person.
>
> OUR HERO: Well then, what about seven months and thirty days? If a fetus is a person at eight months, what about the day before? Is a fetus not a person the day before?
>
> JEAN PAUL: No, it's not.
>
> OUR HERO: What is the difference?
>
> JEAN PAUL: I don't know. I suppose it must be a person at seven months and thirty days.
>
> OUR HERO: What about a week before that? Does something happen in that week to make it a person?
>
> JEAN PAUL: I don't know. No.
>
> OUR HERO: You see, of course, that we can just keep going back and back. You must find a relevant difference between two days, and you can't.

Our Hero has made a good point. There are many other arguments in the abortion debate, but this is one of the most difficult.

The crucial question in judging the slipperiness of a slope is whether the several steps on it are identical. Our Hero here encounters an auto mechanic reluctant to take a moment to fix his car. Notice how Our Hero determines that the mechanic has a good case:

> OUR HERO: Excuse me, but I'm having a bit of trouble.
> GRAHAM: O.K., hang on a moment.
> [After a bit Graham looks at Our Hero's ailing car and informs him it just needs an adjustment to the carburetor, a twenty-minute task.]
> OUR HERO: In that case could you please do it while I wait? It would be a great convenience for me.
> GRAHAM: I'm sorry. There are cars that have been here all day. You'll have to wait your turn. I might not be able to get to it until tomorrow morning.
> OUR HERO: But you said it would only take twenty minutes. Why can't you just do it right away?
> GRAHAM: I can't work like that. It's first come, first served. If I let you get ahead, everyone will want to.
> OUR HERO: But how many people have problems that take only twenty minutes?
> GRAHAM: Quite a few. If I stop to do all of them I'll never get the longer jobs done. You can leave it here or bring it back in the morning, take your pick.

Our Hero determined that Graham was not just being arbitrary, but was faced with a potential flood of delays. Being a fair arguer and convinced that further discussion would be a waste of time, he left. (One way of winning an argument is by knowing when you can save time and just leave.)

The key to winning arguments involving slippery slopes is adherence to the Principle of Similar Cases: is each of the steps exactly the same? The next point is only relevant if the slope is indeed slippery.

There are always two questions to be asked about a slippery slope:

1. Is the slope truly slippery?

2. Should the first step be taken?

If each of the steps is just like the previous one the next question is, *should* the first step be taken? If the slope is slippery and the first step must be taken, there is nothing you can do but enjoy the slide and then come at the problem from another direction. If the first step can be avoided, then you should not take it to begin with. In all cases, always reserve judgment on whether the slope is indeed slippery. In this next example Our Hero grants an assumption about slipperiness only to remind Matt later on that it was a tentative assumption:

> WARE: If a guaranteed minimum income is instituted it will mean the end of this country as we know it.
>
> OUR HERO: How?
>
> WARE: Well, the greatness of this country stems from the industriousness of its people. The guaranteed minimum income will destroy that by eliminating incentive. That, in turn, will put more people on the dole, which will further weaken the work force and increase the burden on the taxpayer. As the burden on working taxpayers increase, they will become more and more discouraged until they finally quit and join the others on the dole. That's how.
>
> HOUR HERO: Let's suppose for the moment your scenario is right. Does that still provide a reason not to have a guaranteed minimum income?
>
> WARE: Well, I for one think those are pretty horrible results.
>
> OUR HERO: I suppose if we couldn't get people to work at all things would be pretty bad.
>
> WARE: Right. It would be pretty awful, wouldn't it?
>
> OUR HERO: It would. But remember, I granted you the whole sequence of events leading to disaster. In fact, I don't think that's what would happen. I don't think the guarantee would destroy incentive. That alone is enough to stop your slippery slope.

The argument will now continue on the new subject: will the guaranteed minimum income destroy incentive? If this is proven by Ware he wins: he has already shown that if his slope is slippery the end follows. Now they will argue about the first step.

The above example provides another reason why listening is important. Frequently, you will be asked to grant an assumption or imagine something is true when you do not really believe it is. This is very common in arguments. But, if you are listening, you will remember what your opposer's claim rests on and can take it back when necessary.

**Always keep track
of what assumptions you have
granted**
for the sake of argument,

**you may want to take one of them
back.**

23 Haste Makes Waste

This section deals with three fallacies all centered on the same theme: jumping to conclusions. The three fallacies, doubtful evidence, mistaken cause, and hasty generalization, all involve moving too quickly from reason to conclusion.

> **A statement needs more than reasons
> for acceptance—**
>
> **it needs good reasons.**

"Doubtful evidence" is a fallacy that is both simple and difficult to avoid. It just involves the use of false or unreasonable evidence. The only real checks against it are investigation and intuition. It often is unrealistic if not impossible to verify statements because the work or information required may be beyond your resources. An excellent instance of this was provided by Ronald Reagan when he described an infamous "welfare chiseler" in Chicago. This woman was alleged by Reagan to be earning over $150,000 in tax-free cash, a figure large enough to make any audience of taxpayers see red. A reporter wondered how anyone could get away with all this, so he decided to investigate. (This of course was the reporter's job; we could not take the time to investigate, and if we did we would not know how to go about it.) It turned out that the charges laid against the woman alleged fraud of only $8,000, not $150,000. And while Reagan had claimed she had eighty aliases, the state charged her with using only four. How could you have known this? How could you have suspected that the information was being exaggerated? There is no real way. The only method available is a defensive attitude.

```
┌─────────────────────────────────────────┐
│ ┌───────────────────────────────────────┐ │
│ │                                       │ │
│ │           Believe nothing.            │ │
│ │                                       │ │
│ └───────────────────────────────────────┘ │
└─────────────────────────────────────────┘
```

The only way to keep from believing false statements is not to believe any statements. By believing nothing you are protecting ourselves. When reading a report in the papers a non-believer will always wonder what is really happening. Most reports in the media are biased in one way or another, so the only reasonable approach is to acquire as much information as possible and sift through it for the common elements and reasonable kernels. These can then be tentatively held for verification, almost believed, or treated as if they were believed. But never be surprised when they turn out false. If you stubbornly refuse to really believe anything you can never go wrong, and those things that you do eventually come to believe stand a better chance of being true. There are many people who really do believe things just because they are in the papers, said by someone famous, or told to them by a supposedly informed source. It is just not safe to believe so much. The next example will illustrate this.

What is written in newspapers may be connected casually to the truth, may be part of the story, or may be wholly fabricated. What the paper says one day may be retracted the next day, or, the denial of whatever charges are made may be buried deep in the body of the article where most readers never wander. Here's a good example: In a newspaper article a while ago a member of the Canadian Parliament was accused of irregularity in election financing. He had received a discount on room rates without declaring it as a donation. At the time there was a lot of concern about such issues. The charge was serious and was placed on the first page. Several days later an article appeared on page three explaining that the politician in question had only used the rooms during the day for resting and changing, and that was why the rate was lower—as it would be for anyone. How many people read the original charges on page one, and how many saw the small item on page three?

One of my favorites was on the front page of the Toronto Star some time ago. The following headline appeared in large type:

ANGOLAN FEMALE FIRING SQUAD
SHOOTS 17 CUBANS FOR RAPE

The first three paragraphs fill in this headline with details that sound like a lead-in from True magazine. The women were supposed to have identified and shot the Cubans. If you read on as far as the fourth paragraph, one paragraph further than most readers go, you learn that the Angolan government has denied the report "with utmost force." What actually happened? We will never know for sure, and certainly never from reading the paper.

If you want to win arguments you must be a Doubting Thomas. Sceptics—
that is, doubters—always have a better chance since they have less to defend.
The more you have to defend, the more there is open to attack. It's as simple as
that. The cost of being a sceptic is no longer having positions on everything.
Most of us have positions on just about every subject under the sun. A sceptic
will frequently answer "I'm not sure" when asked for an opinion. More is
learned by hearing others' beliefs on abortion, education, capital punishment,
sex, religion, politics, you name it. It is true that there are times when you must
make a decision. You have to vote, support issues and so on. At these times you
can sit back, reflect on all the arguments, and hope you decide wisely.

> **Sceptics believe less,
> and so have to defend less.**

The *fallacy of false cause* is similar to doubtful evidence. Reasonable explanations are given, and they could be true, but there is just no reason to think
they are true.

> **Don't think that
> because one thing might be
> a cause of another
> that it is.**

Suppose, for example, that someone states that the cause of poverty is lack
of education. This has a certain appeal to it, a certain air of reasonableness. But
few things have just one cause. Another cause of poverty is lack of jobs. Still
others include poor housing, prejudice, and poor nutrition. Someone else might
say just the opposite and blame a lack of education on poverty. After all, the
poor cannot afford to stay in school, they have to go to work at an early age.

The key to pinpointing a false cause is coming up with another reasonable
cause that is different from the first. Pointing out that it may not be lack of education but prejudice which leads to poverty confuses things; now there are two
equally reasonable explanations. When you do that your opposer may back off
and say that perhaps they are both causes. Your opposer may also choose to defend his or her original reason. In the latter case, the opposer must provide reasons for claiming that one cause and not the other is the important or real one.

> # An explanation is a false-cause fallacy
> ## if other explanations are easily found.

Some time ago someone pointed out that there had been an increase in the incidence of heart disease. At the same time North American consumption of animal fat dropped by 11 percent while consumption of vegetable fat increased by 75 percent. The spokesman pointed out that perhaps the cause of the increase in heart disease was the increased consumption of vegetable fats. This is a classic example of false cause: the simple correlation of two statistics—the decrease in animal fat consumption and the increase in heart disease—is far from sufficing as evidence for one's causing the other. (The spokesman, by the way, was speaking on behalf of the meat industry.)

Another example involving food comes from a bread producer. Preservatives are added to bread to keep it fresh longer. The cause of this, according to a spokesman, is that people don't want their bread going stale in a day. This is undoubtedly true. No one wants bread to go stale in a day. Notice how seductive the fallacy is: the statement itself is true. But the real cause involves the processing of the bread, which removes all the natural ingredients which preserve it. And it may not even be true of mass-produced bread that it does go stale in a day. Finally, anyone who has ever had home-made bread knows that it does not go stale in a day. So blaming our desire for fresh bread is fallacious.

The belief that the use of marijuana leads to the use of heroin is another false cause argument that has been around for a while. Imagine you want to investigate this claim. We go into the field and pay heroin addicts five dollars to fill in some anonymous forms. One of the questions is, "Did you use marijuana before using heroin?" To this 85 percent answer, yes. Leaving aside questions of honesty and so on, you have found a high correlation between heroin use and previous marijuana use. To put it another way, if an individual uses heroin, it is likely he or she previously used marijuana. The big question is, have you established that marijuana use leads to heroin use? Certainly not. There is no information about marijuana users who did not go on to heroin. Today we know that the vast majority of marijuana users never do go on to heroin, but twenty years ago this was not so obvious. Those who knew were not talking.

> **You can always get the results you want,**
> **just ask the right questions**
> **to the right people.**

Another way to illustrate the faulty relationship between the two sets of data is to introduce a third. Suppose you had asked the question, "Did you smoke cigarettes before using heroin?" Again the correlation turns out to be 85 percent. What have you found now? Just as much as before: If you use heroin it is likely that you smoke cigarettes. Changing the example still further, you might question alcoholics about their previous consumption of milk. You would find a tremendously high correlation there. But in this case you know that far more people who drank milk never became alcoholics, so the suggestion is dismissed. But is it not impressive that every alcoholic used to drink milk? It should not be.

> **Attack a false cause in two ways:**
>
> **first, find other causes;**
> **second, find other false correla-**
> **tions.**

These are the best two ways to attack false causes. By coming up with a different reasonable cause we show that there may be other explanations. Next, compare the explanation offered to other simplistic explanations or correlations. A too-simple explanation we all used to believe is that the Civil War was fought to end slavery. Only later in life do we learn the other, economic reasons. Similarly with Columbus's discovery of the New World. The simple, false explanation or cause is that he wanted to prove the world was round. The truth is far more commercial: he was looking for a short, inexpensive trade route to India. These examples do not show that the opposer is wrong, just that causes must be defended.

> **There is not such thing as**
> *the* **cause**
> **of something.**

This last point is what might save anyone so foolish as to claim that one thing is **THE** cause of another. When cornered, you should simply agree that nothing has a unique, single cause. That does not mean one cause is not crucial. "Of course," you magnanimously agree, "nothing is *the* cause of vandalism. Nonetheless, the lack of parental supervision is a contributing factor, don't you think?" Since any unfavorable social condition will encourage vandalism, the statement can hardly prompt disagreement.

The last of the three fallacies in this section is the fallacy of hasty generalization. It is not unusual to hear someone reply to a statement with, "That's just a generalization." But there is no reason to dismiss a statement just because it is a generalization:

> JOSH: Don't believe a word he says—he's running for office, and people running for office make false promises.
> ANNE-LISE: That's a generalization.
> JOSH: So?

Merely pointing out that a statement is general may be interesting, but it hardly provides a reason for dismissing it. Should someone react to one of your statements in this way, reply as Anne-Lise did and wait for an answer.

The explanation for our prejudice against generalizations is the frequency with which they are made too quickly and on poor evidence. They are often far too broad and weeping. In addition, they are easy to knock down: generalizations require only one exception to be proven wrong. The statement that all teachers are afraid of the real world turns out to be false if you can find one teacher who does not have this fear.

> **One exception**
> **falsifies a generalization.**

There is a saying, "it is the exception which proves the rule," that is some-times produced in response to a counter-example. Someone says, as did a letter-writer to a newsmagazine, "Everyone thinks he can get away with anything." Our Hero, who happens to be lurking in a doorway, comes to the rescue:

> OLIVIA: Everyone thinks they can get away with any-thing.
>
> OUR HERO: I don't. If I thought that, I would never pay taxes, for one thing.
>
> OLIVIA: Well, that's just the exception that proves the rule.
>
> OUR HERO: No it isn't. It's the exception that falsifies the generalization.
>
> OLIVIA: Everyone knows there are exceptions to any statement.
>
> OUR HERO: That old saying means just the opposite of what you think. It means that the rule is false if it has excep-tions. The original statement is Scottish and meant the oppo-site of what it sounds like in modern English.
>
> OLIVIA: Well. it's still the case that every generalization has exceptions.
>
> OUR HERO: How many? How much do you want to qualify that statement?
>
> OLIVIA: Most people think they can get away with eve-rything. How's that?
>
> OUR HERO: False. I don't think you're right. Maybe most people think they can get away with *something*, say not paying a parking ticket or something like that; but by and large most people figure they'll be caught if they do anything wrong.
>
> OLIVIA: Well, some people think they can get away with anything.
>
> OUR HERO: That's probably right.

Olivia has been driven back to a much weaker statement. The fallacy of hasty generalization occurs when a statement goes beyond the evidence support-ing it.

Very few statements are universally true, so always put a rider on a state-ment rather than be forced to take it back later. Instead of saying, "All politi-cians are crooks," try this: "An awful lot of politicians are crooks." The latter is a much easier statement to defend.

> **Never make a general statement stronger than you need to—**
>
> **you may be forced to retract.**

We are all familiar with the sorts of qualifiers normally used: "By and large," "just about all...," "most," and so on. these expressions are very vague. "By and large all professors are dull." How many interesting professors are required to make that statement false?

> JUDE: Professors are dull.
> OUR HERO: Do you mean all professors?
> JUDE: No. But most of them are dull.
> OUR HERO: How many is most? 75 percent? 95 percent?
> JUDE: Something like that.
> OUR HERO: How many professors have you known?
> Fifty or Sixty? Maybe you've been unlucky.
> JUDE: That's possible, but I don't think so.
> OUR HERO: Why?

Now Jude is required to defend a statement he probably never meant seriously in the first place. Much to Jude's surprise, Our Hero listened to what he said. Our Hero, knowing that most people speak without thinking, will probably win this argument easily. The key to winning, as always, is listening.

24. Three Sneaky Moves

The last three fallacies to be presented are the fallacy of false dilemma, the fallacy of two wrongs or common practice, and the fallacy of appeal to force. They are all common maneuvers and should be high on your list of tactics to watch for.

A dilemma is a situation in which you must make a choice. Very often there is no difficulty at all in making choices, while at other times the decision can be quite a problem. Usually, saying that someone is in a dilemma means she must make a difficult choice. In fact all choices are dilemmas, but we tend to save the name for the hard ones. The question now is, when is a dilemma a "false dilemma"? Put another way the answer is obvious: when is a decision between two alternatives phony? Answer: when there are really more than two alternatives.

> ## Be suspicious of choices:
>
> ## are there really more
> ## than you have been offered?

A false dilemma is a maneuver that attempts to limit the number of choices in a given situation. A very famous slogan of the Vietnam era, "America—Love it or Leave It," was based on a false dilemma. Why are loving and leaving the only two choices? Surely there are others. Observe Emma try to con Our Hero.

> EMMA: Excuse me, sir. Would you care to sign this petition?
> OUR HERO: What's it about?
> EMMA: It demands the government make cigarette smoking illegal.

OUR HERO: Well, I don't think I will sign, thank you.

EMMA: Oh, so you don't care who gets cancer?

OUR HERO: Are those your only alternatives: either sign or you're in favor of cancer?

EMMA: What if they are?

OUR HERO: It's a lousy argument, that's what. There are many people including myself who are not smokers but would not sign your petition. You are just offering a false dilemma.

Emma may not be impressed by this attack, but Our Hero is correct: the alternatives have been unfairly limited to two. There are many others.

It is very common when false dilemmas are introduced to have one of the two choices be the obvious favorite. This is usually done by phrasing the two alternatives in highly leading language. There was a heated debate a while ago in Toronto concerning the musical *Showboat*. Some groups claimed that the show was racist and should not be supported by public funds, and that no one ought go see the show. Some said that anyone who did buy a ticket was racist, so either you boycotted the show or you were a racist. What a choice! There are many alternatives between the two laid out. One might believe the show is not racist, or that it was but is historically important, or that such shows must be seen and understood in context. It can easily be seen why this fallacy is sometimes called the fallacy of black-and-white. Everything is put into final one-or-the-other terms.

Political parties, whether in power or out, often use the fallacy of false dilemma to try and frighten people. "Either support us or suffer terrible consequences." The National Rifle Association keeps claiming that either citizens have easy access to firearms, or the U.S. will be controlled by criminals. One alternative has people running around with everything from derringers to machineguns, and the other has a defenseless population cowering fearfully in their bedrooms. Is there nothing between the two? What about stricter controls that do not completely eliminate gun ownership? What about limiting ownership to police forces and increasing penalties for carrying illegal firearms? These are all possibilities that the dilemma tries to ignore.

Another example frequently occurs in debates that pit ecological issues against economic concerns. The green side claims that unless the environment is completely protected and left untouched we will all perish like the dinosaurs. On the other side, industrialists and developers point to the children of unemployed workers who will starve or be on welfare unless the forests and the oceans are denuded. The choices you are given are the destruction of the planet or the ruination of a community. No wonder it's a hard argument. Remember, in the fight for your opinion, the fallacy of false dilemma is a potent weapon.

> # When the choices seem extreme
> # look in the middle.

The next fallacy is "two wrongs," or "common practice." In this fallacy the justification for bad actions is that others do it. An argument that always seems to bring out this fallacy concerns corporate bribery in foreign countries. Executives argue that when doing business in many countries it is necessary to use bribes because that is what is done there. Unless we do it too, they argue, we'll lose business and jobs. This statement incorporates a fallacy: the argument against bribery is that bribery is wrong. The counter-argument is irrelevant to the original statement. The fact that everyone does it is not enough to make it right.

> # Replies appealing to common
> # practice
> # are almost always
> # irrelevant.

Another sort of appeal justifies something wrong by pointing to something else that is also wrong. A boss might refuse a reasonable request for a raise by pointing out that several employees were recently laid off. How would it look if you were given a raise when other were laid off? This is the fallacy of two wrongs. It was unfortunate that others were laid off, but that is not really relevant to your raise. (It would be relevant if the boss pointed out that there simply was no money, but that was not the argument.) Some (but not all) arguments for affirmative action defend discrimination against men on the grounds that there is discrimination against women. There are other, non-fallacious arguments that depend on the notions of historical redress and the need to correct current imbalances. But, defending discrimination against men simply because there is discrimination against women is like defending violence against men because there is violence against women. More violence doesn't help anyone.

The next dialogue also illustrates the fallacy.

> OLIVIA: The police must be given broader powers to stop organized crime.
>
> OUR HERO: While I would like to see organized crime stopped, I'm afraid the powers might be abused.
>
> OLIVIA: You can't make an omelette without breaking a few eggs. Some people might be hurt, but that can't be helped.
>
> OUR HERO: I think that requires some defense, Olivia. What's the point of stopping crime if people will be hurt? After all, we want to stop crime because it hurts people.
>
> OLIVIA: Fewer people will be hurt by the police than by criminals.
>
> OUR HERO: I think that's true. But if anyone is hurt by the police it's wrong. If we remove rights, we have changed the whole system we are trying to protect in the first place. Two wrongs do not make a right: just because the crooks are doing nasty things does not mean that we should.

This argument is liable to continue for some time. Simply pointing out that a fallacy is committed may not stop your opposer: the reason for abandoning the argument must be presented. Our Hero is correct that the argument is a two-wrongs fallacy. Olivia may still have a chance to make her case if she thinks quickly, though I would bet on Our Hero. Our Hero might, for example, point out that Olivia's solution is like eliminating poverty by shooting all the poor people—it is a solution, but at what cost?

Another form of the fallacy argues that while an action is not good, it is not as bad as some other action. In a letter to the editor a reader argued that industrialized countries have no right to protest the destruction of the Brazilian rain forests. Why? Because we also cut down trees here in North America. But even if the scale were the same, the fact that trees are being cut in North America does not mean they should be cut everywhere. That would be like saying that since many big bank robbers get away with their crimes, we should be allowed to hold up corner stores. The commission of one evil does not permit the commission of another.

> ### The use of "two wrongs" is an admission of guilt.

In this dialogue the above tip is demonstrated by Our Hero.

LAUREN: Certainly violence is justified when the revolutionary aims are valuable.

OUR HERO: But won't innocent people get hurt?

LAUREN: That may happen. But remember, the existing government is also hurting innocent people.

OUR HERO: Is that one reason you oppose them?

LAUREN: Certainly. The revolution will benefit those now being hurt.

OUR HERO: As you've already said that innocent people will be hurt, and that is one reason for your revolution, how can you possibly justify actions that will lead to the same evil? You are saying since they do it, you can do it as well. Yet at the same time you claim to be better than they are. That's confusing.

You can have doubts as to Our Hero's revolution-stopping capabilities—not because he argues poorly, but because Lauren may not argue well.

Common practice is often used to justify little wrongs such as taking stationery home from work. Everyone does it, so why shouldn't we do it? The fact that everyone does it is irrelevant. It is the nature of the act, the degree of wrong that accounts for our attitude, not how common it is. In some places, for example, vandalism is quite common, yet people still know it is wrong.

JEAN PAUL: Don't buy a pen. I can get you one from my office.

OUR HERO: That's stealing.

JEAN PAUL: No, don't be silly. Everyone takes stuff home from the office.

OUR HERO: I know, but it's stealing.

JEAN PAUL: It's more like a fringe benefit.

OUR HERO: Oh, then you declare it on your income taxes?

JEAN PAUL: Of course not. Look...

OUR HERO: Wait. Do you do it openly in front of your boss or co-workers?

JEAN PAUL: No. That's now how it's done.

OUR HERO: Sounds like stealing to me.

JEAN PAUL: Everyone does it.

OUR HERO: O.k., so we agree that everyone steals. I just don't know if it's such a good idea.

Now Jean Paul and Our Hero have something to argue about: is petty theft something that is wrong? That argument might end up either way, and it should be a good one. Notice that Our Hero first tackled the job of getting office theft classed as stealing. This is valuable since calling it by any other name would confuse the issue. Also notice that if Our Hero were to continue the argument, or rather try to end it, with something like, "Well then, since stealing is wrong, what you're doing is wrong," Jean Paul would be wise to jump on him for begging the question. Having the activity classed as stealing does not automatically mean that it is wrong. (Imagine someone stealing a murderer's gun: that would certainly not be wrong.)

The last fallacy is appeal to force, known in Latin circles as the argumentum ad baculum. Any threat to loss of life, health, wealth, freedom, and so on is an appeal to force. The basis of an appeal to force is fear. It might be to fear of the unknown, as in religious appeals; it might be to fear of foreigners, as in patriotic appeals; or it might be to fear of harm or danger, as in many perfectly reasonable appeals. In other words, not every appeal to force is improper. If you are about to embark on a voyage in a leaky ship and someone says you ought not go because you will drown, we have an appeal to force through the fear of death. When a mugger says, "Your money or your life," there is also an appeal to force which most of us would respect.

> **A threat is never a good reason to believe something,**
>
> **but it may be a good reason to do something.**

In other words, the mugger does not deserve the money, but you should give it to him nonetheless. An employee arguing with his boss over the company donation to the annual picnic is perfectly correct in watching for the darkening of visage and drawing of brows indicating loss of temper. As the issue gathers importance he may want to push things further, but always remember that you are usually better off returning to the fray with new arguments, new data and your job still secure.

An appeal to force is fallacious because it ignores what is right and wrong, true or false. Using threats comes down to saying no more arguments, no more investigations, the case is closed. But the case is never closed because nothing is ever certain. The expression "power politics" has a very nice ring to it, but it refers to arguments from force. According to author Philip Deane, When Lyndon Johnson was president he once used this argument to convince the Greek Ambassador to favor a U.S. proposal about Cyprus. Deane quotes Johnson as follows: "[Obscenity] your Parliament and Constitution. America is an elephant. Cyprus is a flea. Greece is a flea. If those two fleas continue itching the ele-

phant, they might just get whacked by the elephant's Trunk, whacked good."
Even if the Ambassador does not like the U.S. proposal this threat may yet persuade him to accept Johnson's point of view. The argument is fallacious since
the threat has nothing to do with the proposal. Nor has politics changed in more
recent times. Military might has been used to end arguments in Haiti, Rwanda,
Somalia, and Irag.

Personal relationships, like diplomatic relations between countries, sometimes involves threats of varying kinds. The greatest difficulty with using force
as an argument is that it achieves only a temporary victory. As soon as the threat
of force is removed, the opponent will go back to his original position, often
with renewed fervor.

> **Force may end an argument—**
>
> **but the result will not endure.**

Even countries who often use the threat of force find themselves with fickle
partners and precarious victories that constantly require attention and vigilance.
When this is done in personal argumentation the results can be not only disas-
torous, but tiring and isolating as well.

Fears are very easy things to prey on. We all feel insecure about our intel-
lectual, social, and sexual prowess. By feeding on these more or less hidden
fears advertising is able to persuade us through totally irrelevant reasons. We
purchase cars that are expensive and flashy, cosmetics that will make us sexy
and attractive, and furnishings that will enhance our prestige. Ads for Scotch
whiskey point out that people will notice what brand you serve: you dare not
serve the inferior brand lest people suppose you cannot afford better.

> **When looking at an advertisement**
> **always ask yourself,**
>
> **what is the ad really selling?**

In most cases what is being touted in the ad is irrelevant to the actual product. An ad for Old Grand-Dad whiskey stated in huge letters: "If not for your-

self, for your image." No matter what the stuff tastes like you should still use it! Another ad for Bushmills Irish Whiskey simply pointed out that, "You can tell a lot about an individual by what he pours into his glass." (You can also tell a lot by how much he pours in his glass, but the ad says nothing about that.) Cosmetics ads with sexual suggestions also give irrelevant reasons: there is no claim that the product will do anything, but the whole ad conveys a sexual feeling. These techniques mean that we must be very careful in reading advertisements. Age is one of the strongest advertising cudgels around these days. No one wants to get old, and the advertisers know this and prey on our fear of ageing. Whether you like it or not, you are affected by these ads. Since their appeal is largely unconscious, you cannot help it.

When a threat is made, explicitly or implicitly, think before being frightened.

Is the threat

something to be feared?

Once, many of us were afraid of ghosts; after all, they are scary. Many of our fears are just as poorly founded, so think before accepting this fallacy.

25. Section II Review

Questions

What fallacy, if any, do you see in the following examples, and what should the next step be?

1.   "So now," Arnie said, "The schools are encouraging young kids to have sex."
"What? They are?" Carole replied.
"Sure they're supplying them with condoms and instructions on how to use them. Next thing they'll be giving them beds."

2.   "Violence on television is rampant," Larry said. "It's permeating our society and teaching our kids all the wrong things."
"So you're suggesting, like, censorship or something?" Peggy asked.
"It's got to be stopped. I mean, don't you think there's too much violence in our society?'
"Well, there sure is. It's getting worse and worse all the time."
"You see, that's exactly my point."

3.   ROBERT: Of course the Mayor wants the new subway built along Goatherd Avenue, he and all his friends own a lot of property there.
STEVE: I didn't know that.
ROBERT: Well, you may be the only left who doesn't. I mean, there's no other reason to pick that street, right?

4.   PETER: So, boss, am I getting the promotion or not?
BOSS: No, I'm afraid, Peter, that you were not our first choice for the promotion.
PETER: But why not? I thought I was a strong candidate.
BOSS: We just felt you weren't right for the job.

5.   "Look at the lineup for that restaurant," Sharon said, "let's try it next Saturday for our anniversary."

6.   "I knew it," Shirley cried, her eyes brimming with tears, "you don't love me! You never did!"

"What are you talking about?" Alex asked, thoroughly perplexed. "Of course I love you. Aren't I taking you to the prom?"

"If you loved me you never would have forgotten."

"Forgotten? Forgotten what?"

Shirley wells over with emotion and a huge sob escapes: "Today's our three month anniversary, and you didn't remember!"

7.   "Good gosh," Sean exclaimed, "did you see what those people were eating?"

"Yes. It looked like muck with chicken beaks in it," Shiela agreed.

"It just goes to show what kind of people they are."

"Too true. Now let's hurry home for lunch. I think there's some leftover haggis in the fridge."

8.   "I never said that!"

"Oh, yes you did!"

"I did not. I would never say anything like that."

"You said it. In fact you said it twice. And the second time you were shouting!"

"It's not true. I never said it. And you're the one who's shouting."

"I am not shouting. You are. You're always shouting."

"I never shout. You're the one who always shouts first."

"That's a lie...

9.   John Drache has a computer problem. He can't figure out how to get his new printer to work. He complains to Joan, a co-worker, and she advises him to check his word processor to see if the correct printer is listed. John unhesitatingly takes her advice.

10.   "I don't know how you can take that astrology garbage seriously. Here, look at this. One of the world's greatest astronomers, a Nobel Prize winner, was interviewed and called astrology a load of hooey."

Answers

1.   The fallacy of **straw man** occurs when a position is exaggerated beyond what it's proponents hold. Anyone one who wants condoms supplied in schools would explain that they are just being realistic, not promoting sex.

2.   But, of course, it wasn't his point. What's happend here is the **fallacy of *non sequitor*,** a quick change of subject. Larry, perhaps unintentionally, got off the tricky matter of censorship and onto the safer ground of anti-violence.

3.   If you picked ***argumentum ad hominem***, then you were right. Robert's first claim that the mayor owns property along the proposed route must be shown to be relevant. And, if you picked ***argumentum ad populum***, then you are also correct. Robert bolsters his claim by stating that "everyone knows" about the scam. That might be just another way of saying he believes it. Finally, if you selected the **fallacy of false dilemma** you found the last fallacy. There are undoubtedly other reasons in favor of the route, but Robert's not interested in hearing them. Moral: 1] there can be more than one fallacy in even a brief argument, and 2] watch out for Robert if you run into him.

4.   Peter asked a straightforward question and received a straightforward answer. But when peter followed through with a request for reasons, he did not get one. Saying that he's not "right for the job" is just another way of saying he didn't get it. This is the **fallacy of begging the question**, and Peter's best response is to ask why he's not "right for the job".

5.   Sharon was wrong: the food wasn't good at all. The crowds came to see the ex-football player who owned the place. Her mistake was to fall for the ***argumentum ad populum***, the fallacy that because something is popular it is good or true.

6.   While Shirley may or may not be justified in her disappointment with Alex's forgetfulness, her assumption about his lack of love for her is a **hasty conclusion**.

7.   When we think we are somehow better than others we commit the **fallacy of provincialism**. Every culture produces food that are treated as delicacies by insiders and appalling by outsiders.

8.   In arguments like this one, sadly familiar to many of us, one of the biggest problems is the constant changing of subjects. The ***non sequitors*** flow like water. Let's hope that things will eventually simmer down and the real issues will be broached.

9.   One might suspect an *ad verecundiam*, appeal to authority has been committed, but it has not. On everyday matters it is perfectly appropriate to take the advice of someone who knows more than you do. Even if your only evidence is that they sound like they know what they're talking about. Joan might, after all, save John a trip to the computer store.

10. First of all, it is *not* a fallacious appeal to authority. An expert in astronomy is entitled to have an opinion on astrology which is worth attending to. What it might be, is a **circular argument**, but what it really is is a good reason to question astrology. By the way, what's your sign?

Part III

THE ARGUMENTS

26. Pot Luck

Paul: Lord, I wish they'd legalize marijuana already.

Chris: Are you sure that's a good idea?

> *Good. Chris responds to Paul's statement with a question, not with another statement. This is the right way.*

Paul: Sure I'm sure. Don't tell me you think it should be illegal. You must be the last person in the world to believe that.

> *Paul is trying to intimidate Chris: being the last person to agree means being "out of it". This is a fallacy. Notice that Paul has not yet given a reason for his position.*

Chris: If I'm the last person how come it's still illegal? I'd like to know why it should legal. After all, there's no proof it isn't harmful.

> *Good. This is an excellent response to the fallacy.*

> *Mistake. Chris has offered a reason when he did not have to— he did not start the argument. If Paul attacks, Chris may be on the defensive..*

Paul: How much proof is needed? Marijuana must be the most tested drug in history. They've been trying to find something wrong with it for years. Why should that drug need more testing than anything else?

Chris: Because it is taken for pleasure, not out of necessity. Other drugs are needed for health, not highs.

> *Chris is solidly on the defensive. He should be ending his answers with questions in order to get Paul on the defensive.*

Paul: So what? What does the purpose matter? Are you saying no drugs should be used for pleasure?

Chris: They should be used as little as possible altogether. It just isn't a good idea to put foreign substances into our bodies. When it comes to medicine it may be necessary. But why risk health for pleasure?

> *Paul has identified Chris's principle (drugs are bad), and Chris has agreed.*

Paul: What about alcohol? That's a drug used for pleasure, and it's legal.

> *Paul is appealing to the Principle of Similar Cases.*

Chris: I personally don't think it should be legal. I would make booze illegal rather than make grass illegal.

> *Good. Any other answer would have led to trouble. Trying to distinguish between alcohol and marijuana would be hard.*

Paul: But you drink!

> *Oops. Paul made a statement and did not ask a question. Chris may be able to grab the offensive.*

Chris: So what?

Paul: I suppose that's not important. don't you think the choice to protect our bodies from all these chemicals and so on should be personal?

> *Bravo. Paul realized he made a mistake. More important, he realized it does not matter that Chris drinks. Rather than try to defend his point he quickly gave it up and moved on to more fruitful fields. Chris should have made his attack stronger.*

Chris: Because one function of society is to protect its members.

Paul: To what degree? I'm delighted that poison can't be sold as vitamins, and that milk must be clean. But surely we must be allowed some choices. Why not make candy illegal?

> *There is a new principle (that society must protect its members), so Paul needs a new counter-example. He wants to show that Chris does not really accept that principle.*

Chris: Don't be silly.

> *A reply like this means that Chris cannot think of an answer. It is a signal for Paul to move in.*

Paul: I'm not being silly. Candy is bad for us. It rots our teeth, makes us fat, keeps us from eating properly, and contains dozens of artificial things. Not only that, but the main users are children. Think of it, Chris, children. Why shouldn't we make it illegal?

Chris: Candy is different. I agree that chemicals in it should be taken out, but it's in a different class.

Paul: But you still haven't told me how candy is different. Why should one thing that's bad be legal and another illegal?

Chris: I don't know. I just hate the idea of legalizing another way of damaging our bodies. Why should we increase the number of bad things?

Paul: I don't think we are increasing the number of bad things. I don't think grass is bad. You want to penalize one segment of society because the stuff they like came along later than booze and candy. That's just not fair.

> *Chris has still not pointed to a difference between candy and marijuana.*

> *Good. Paul noticed that Chris did not answer the question.*

> *Chris has lost. He cannot make the distinction. There may be one, but Chris cannot find it, and knows he is in trouble. Since he has no defense, he tries to take the offense by asking a question. He is also accusing Paul of committing the fallacy of two wrongs make a right.*

> *Paul rejects Chris's charge by denying grass is bad. He remembers that was an assumption implicit in the argument, not an agreed upon fact. Chris, borrowed the fact that marijuana is bad, it was not proven.*

27. The Gay Life

Jacob: Did you read about that guy who was drummed out of the army for being an open homosexual?

Daniel: Yeah. I'd like to see more of that. This whole business of it being all right is nuts. Did you think he shouldn't have been kicked out?

Jacob: Gee, it's not nearly so clear to me. What makes you so sure the army is right?

> Good. All too often we defend a position we are not really sure of. This always tends to lead to trouble. We are much better off saying we are not sure and letting the opposer carry the ball.

Daniel: Well, I just think it's getting to the point where we have to do something or our kids will end up thinking it's normal to be queer. You don't want your kids to be queer, do you?

Jacob: Well, I guess I rather they weren't gay. What bothers me is the connection. You seem so sure about these kids becoming gay. Why?

Daniel: Don't be naive, Jacob. Even the President backed down on it. Would he risk changing his mind if he weren't convinced?

> Daniel's intimidating question incorporated an appeal to fear. Jacob handles it well here by not giving it a big play.

> This is the fallacy of appealing to authority. The President is not an expert on homosexuality, only on popular opinion.

Jacob: Maybe, and maybe not. But I need persuading. I can't see taking away someone's rights without a damn good reason. The next thing you know they'll go after bachelors.

Daniel: come off it! What are you talking about?

Jacob: Look, the army says it can fire this guy because he's queer. Well, that means they're firing him because of what he does with some other people on his own time. So what's to stop them from firing me for sleeping with women?

Daniel: Why would they do that?

> *Jacob is not getting anywhere. His next move is to bring his point home by applying it to a case Daniel will care about. He also handled the fallacy of authority very nicely.*

> *Now Jacob has made his point clearly, so it is a good time for a question. Daniel will have to deal with Jacob's argument sooner or later.*

> *Daniel did not see a quick answer, so he replied with a question. This is about the best move there is when a response is needed.*

Jacob: Maybe because there's a lot more women in the army now. It doesn't really matter. If they can throw this guy out, what about me? And you don't stay home alone every night yourself, my boy.

Daniel: There are laws to stop that sort of thing. It doesn't make sense to firs someone for sleeping with a girlfriend, everyone does it.

> *There are to separate fallacies in this response. The first is begging the question: Why shouldn't the laws protecting heterosexual couples also protect homosexual couples? The second fallacy is common practice: the fact that everyone sleeps with his girlfriend does not make it right.*

Jacob: Well, then, why aren't there laws to stop homosexuals from being fired? A lot of people are gay.

Daniel: That's different. It's not normal.

Jacob: Maybe it isn't the norm, but is it wrong/ Are guys getting fired for no good reason?

> *Jacob does not want to argue about the meaning of "normal" and neatly avoids the issue. His use of the hedge expression "maybe" means that he can retract the statement later if he needs to.*

Daniel: Look, Jake, the more acceptance of gays there is the more chance there is the kids will get turned on to it. That's the thing that really worries me.

Jacob: But the psychologists say that a kids sexual orientation is set by the time he's five. That's before a lot of contact out of the home. How about that?

Daniel: That's fine for them. Maybe they don't have kids.

Anyway, the shrinks are the ones always letting killers out of jail, aren't they?

> This statement is completely irrelevant. Having kids has nothing to do with expertise.

> This is slightly better since it reflects on the reliability of psychologists.

Jacob: We're getting nowhere fast, Daniel. We don't even know if the guy had anything to do with kids. If he didn't, do you still think he should be fired?

Daniel: Well, I suppose in the army he wouldn't have a lot of contact with kids, so maybe he shouldn't be fired. But gays shouldn't be allowed near kids.

> Notice that Jacob is not conceding the point with his question. All he is doing is trying to clarify and narrow the argument. The issue will now depend on Daniel's answer.

Jacob: Why not? What are they going to do? Do you think all gays are child molesters?

Daniel: Probably not, but it wouldn't shock me. What I'm afraid of is the kids imitating them. Teachers, for instance, have a great effect on kids. If that would make a difference, then I say fire them.

> Now that one route has been selected it can be examined more closely.

Jacob: Well, I don't know enough about that. We need some experts there, I guess. But still, by whose lights would the effect be bad?

Daniel: My lights. Frankly, Jacob, the whole idea scares the hell out of me. I don't care if it is wrong, I want it done and I'm not willing to argue about it.

> Neither disputant is able to argue the technical points, so they will move on to the more general issue.

> It is a good technique to announce when argument will no longer help. It is fair to your opposer and keeps the argument from getting too heated.

Jacob: All right, my friend, I won't push the point. I'm just worried that you're being paranoid and unfair.

> *Jacob is respecting Daniel's desire to stop. He leaves Daniel with a thought that neatly captures the main point.*

28. Equal Rights for Equal Arguments

Krista: I decided to apply for the policewoman's job.

Mark: What? I think you're nuts.

Krista: Nuts? Why am I nuts?.

> *Good. Instead of reacting Krista treats the "nuts" statement like a claim.*

Mark: Women don't belong on the police force. I mean, they can't go running after robbers and muggers, can they?

Krista: Why not?

> *Still the right move. The temptation to immediately go on the attack is very strong. But it should be resisted. By asking a question Krista gets a better idea of what to attack.*

Mark: Heh, heh. Who'd save the cops from the bad guys?

> *Mark has not said anything new; he is just repeating what he said already. His comments should not be treated as a reason, but as a conclusion. Krista's response is correct.*

Krista: What makes you think that would happen?

Mark: Come on, Krista. Most men could make mincemeat of most women. How can women be expected to subdue criminals and arrest them?

Krista: You think men would have an easier time arresting criminals than women would? Is that right?

Mark: Exactly, I just can't see how...

Krista: Wait. I want to get straight on this. If I can convince you that a woman can have as easy a time as a man in an arrest situation, then you'll agree?

Mark: Sure. You convince me that any woman will have as easy a time and you're in.

Krista: No. Not any woman. any woman who wants to be a cop and meets the requirements. After all, there are lots of guys who would have trouble arresting a kid.

Mark: O.K., you're on.

[Krista reaches over to Mark, grabs his are and flips him over. He ends up on the floor, and Krista has a firm hammer lock on him. Since this conversation is taking place in New York, no one else in the bar has noticed.]

Mark: What the hell! You're crazy! Get off me!

Krista: Well, do you agree a woman can arrest a man?

Mark: No! I don't! Just because you threw me doesn't mean I have to agree. You took me by surprise. I agree you threw me, but that doesn't mean a woman can throw a man whenever she wants. I wasn't ready.

Krista: Are you ready now?

Mark: No! Don't! I admit you can throw me whenever you want to, but that's still doesn't make the point.

> *Krista wants the argument to be precise. The best way to do this is to get the agreement of your opposer on the issue.*

> *A good interruption. Mark was likely just going to repeat himself again. A very powerful move, and one that attempts to make the rules of the game perfectly clear.*

> *Mark, intentionally or not, distorted Krista's position. Krista noticed the straw man fallacy and reacted.*

> *This is known as nonverbal communication. Krista has demonstrated a fact, but which fact is still open to debate.*

> *Good. Mark recovered his wits, and he is not letting Krista make a hasty generalization.*

Krista: Oh, but mark, it does. Don't you see? Why can I throw you? I'm not bigger than you.

> *Emotion is not out of place in an argument so long as the issues are kept in sight. Showing concern, excitement, or anger is fine if it does not interfere with the discussion.*

Mark: Because you're a bloody black belt in karate, that's why. Besides, you're mad. What would you do if you ran up against a crook who also studied karate?

> *This is a sign of retreat. By his question Mark shows he agrees that women could win if trained.*

Krista: The same thing a male cop would do—call for help. The point is we can be on the same footing.

Mark: Women cops, you know, would lead to more violence. There's no question about it.

> *A dramatic change of subject.*

Krista: What? Why?

> *Oh, no. Krista did not react to the switch. She may be interested in what Mark said, but she should have tied up the argument first.*

Mark: Well, men have always been the enforcement figures. It is easier for us to obey men since most of us were obedient to fathers. The cop on the beat has a whole historical tradition and psychology to back him up. That's why he survives as well as he does. Women don't have that tradition, so they are more likely to get attacked. When that happens they'll have to use force and guns more often themselves. See what I mean?

> *A clever move by Mark. His argument is long enough to make his recent loss just a memory, and it is complex enough so Krista will have to concentrate on what he is saying.*

Krista: What sort of drugstore psychology is that? As soon as it is understood that women are not going to take crap when they're cops, they'll have all the respect they need.

> *This is the fallacy of attacking the person. It is not serious, though, because it is followed by reasons.*

Mark: But how many people will be hurt while they earn that respect? Anyway, it sounds more like fear to me.

> *Mark is sticking to his point: other people will suffer if women are allowed to be cops on the beat.*

Krista: Mark, that's just the point. Maybe it's necessary to hurt some people in order to get the idea across that women can do anything. It shouldn't be necessary to earn respect, but it is. Does that mean we have to stay home and cook? It's not our fault women aren't respected. Why should we suffer for it?

> *A good reply to the core of Mark's point. Krista tags a question Mark cannot answer.*

Mark: Well, I just hope you never have to arrest me, that's all.

> *Mark is admitting defeat. Krista must not demand more of a victory. To insist that our opposers stand up and agree they have lost is a mistake. Any resentment created by such a demand is liable to interfere with persuasion. We must always keep in mind the point of arguing: persuasion.*

A general point: Krista missed a switch in the subject. Had she not won the subsequent argument her first victory might have been forgotten. Always wrap up one part of an argument before changing topics.

29. Why Get Married?

Zachary: Why get married? I don't see the point.

Jennifer: I told you why. It's a way of expressing commitment.

Zack: I have no qualms about expressing commitment. I've told you over and over that we will be together forever. But why get married?

> Zack has accepted the idea that commitment is important. Now the argument should be about the form of the commitment.

Jen: I know you've said it. But I guess that isn't enough.

Zack: We've been living together for two years. Doesn't that count as a sign?

Jen: Sure, but I still want to get married.

Zack: What difference would it make? Nothing would change. It's just a piece of paper.

Jen: If that's true, why not get married?

> Good. After all, Zack is saying it is no big deal, so...

Zack: Because I don't like going along with the system, that's why.

> This could be trouble for Zachary. Notice how the offense has switched to Jennifer. She is now asking the questions, while he is providing the answers. If he runs out of answers he may be married.

Jen: Nonsense. You work in a law firm, you belong to clubs, you vote, you go along with the system right down the line.

> *This is a direct rebuttal that makes use of counter-examples. Zachary must now provide a different reason, or show why the examples are not like marriage.*

Zack: Those are different. I *have* to work, and if I don't vote then I'm not getting a say. If we get married we'll end up like everybody else. I wish I knew what was going on with you.

Jen: There's nothing secret going on with me. I'm spending a lot of years with you, and I want to know that we really are planning to do this forever. The best way I know of saying that is, "I do."

> *Jennifer is wise to put her case on the level of feelings. Trying rational argument would not work.*

Zack: You always get so extreme about things.

> *This is a desperate attempt to change the subject.*

Jen: Did you hear what I just said?

Zack: Of course.

Jen: What did I say? Tell me.

> *This is a good way of forcing an issue.*

Zack: You said you're worried about the future. Right?

Jen: Right. I want to know that you are as committed as I am. You haven't given me one reason for not getting married.

Zack: That's not true. I've given lots.

Jen: Why don't you tell me what's really going on? What are you really feeling?

> *The fact that the argument is going nowhere is a good sign that feelings and emotions may be involved. Jennifer is correct to stop going in circles and to try to get to the real issues.*

Zack: If you really want to know, the idea of getting married scares the hell out of me. It just frightens me to death.

At this point there should be a discussion between Jen and Zack about their feelings toward marriage. The rational façade was dismissed through argument.

No one really has good arguments one way or the other. What they have to do is begin talking about what they feel.

30. Good-bye, Friends

Jason: Hi, Matt. I just came by to say so long.

Matt: Where are you going? I had no idea you were leaving.

Jason: I'm joining the Star people. I move in with them tomorrow.

Matt: What! You're leaving your house? What about your job?

Jason: No. I'm keeping my job, but I'm selling my house and giving the money to the Stars. They need it more than I do. I'm also afraid we won't be able to have lunch together again.

Matt: You're mad! This is crazy! They're taking you for a ride! Have you thought about this?

Jason: We Star people believe thinking is wrong. Feeling is all that matters. I feel this is right for me.

> *This outrageously begs the question. By what process does Jason know thinking is wrong?*

> *Good. Matt stresses agreement.*

Matt: Jason, I like feeling too. I think feeling is great. But how can you trust your feelings all the time? What if they're wrong?

Jason: Feelings just are. There's no question of right or wrong.

Matt: Sometimes I feel like I should kill my wife. I get incredibly angry and full of homicidal feelings. That doesn't mean I should even harm her.

> *Matt is testing Jason's principle. Jason's answer will indicate if it is "follow all feeling."*

Jason: You just have those feelings because you are impure. You don't understand that the only real feeling is love.

Matt: Love is the only feeling? That's the only thing you ever feel?

Jason: Right, Matt. It's beautiful and peaceful.

Matt: What about hate, fear, jealousy, desire, annoyance, exasperation? Don't you ever feel any of those?

Jason: No.

Matt: Sounds boring. You really don't feel anger anymore? If I socked you one you'd just grin at me? How do you protect yourself?

Jason: There is no need to.

Matt: What about fear? Without fear you might walk off a cliff or something.

Jason: You don't need fear to avoid that, just sense. No, love is all that's needed.

Matt: Let's leave love alone for a minute. You said you're selling your house and giving them the money, right?

Jason: right. I give up my house and two-thirds of my salary.

Matt: I should've guessed. Why do they need all that money?

Jason: It's mostly used for missions to gain converts. We want the whole world bathed in love. But the other thing is liberating ourselves from material possessions. By giving up my worldly attachments I can get closer to reality and see its love.

Matt: If there are many people in your income bracket involved, we're talking about a hefty sum of money. Who gets all this loot? Someone must be making a good living out of this.

> *This does get Jason out of trouble— but it love the only feeling?*

> *Matt is going wrong. He should not try to argue about Jason's newfound insights. This won't get anywhere.*

> *If one avenue of attack is not working, try another.*

> *Good. Jason gives two answers— if one does not work, the other may.*

Jason: You really don't understand, Matt. You see everything in commercial terms.

Matt: You're not being very open-minded, Jason. If I disagree you say I don't understand. That's not a great attitude for someone whose only feeling is love. I just want to know what's going on.

Jason: I'm sorry, Matt, but you can't really know. You have to feel it, not understand it.

> *This dismisses Matt's comment without a reason, so it's a fallacy.*

> *The fallacy of special pleading was just committed. It is claimed that anyone who does not have this special characteristic cannot understand.*

Matt: Look, Jason, I feel very bad about this. I'm really all torn up and I want you to try and help me. O.K.?

Jason: If it's help you want, I'll give it.

Matt: You know I feel you're being ripped off and hoodwinked. Can you understand how I feel?

Jason: sure. It's difficult with something strange.

Matt:: O.K., here's my pitch. Is it possible you are wrong? I mean is it remotely, distantly, somehow possible that you're being conned?

Jason: No, Matt, it isn't.

Matt: You don't understand, Jason. I mean is it *possible*; I'm not saying you're wrong. I just want to know if it's possible that somewhere a mistake was made? I mean, nothing is certain in life, is it? You might be wrong? You don't think you are, but you might be?

Jason: I suppose it's possible. But it isn't true; I'm not being taken by anyone for anything.

Matt: How would you know if you were? What would change your mind?

> *Matt is going to try another tack. He sees his line and wants to be sure that Jason will be listening.*

> *Matt must keep at this question until he gets a yes.*

> *Matt can keep asking this until Jason is exhausted.*

> *The next step requires Jason to agree to what evidence is needed.*

Jason: I don't know. what are you getting at?

Matt: What if I prove that some of the higher-ups in this organization are making a lot of money for themselves? If I could show that, would you reconsider?

Jason: Well, I don't know.

Matt: You keep saying that, Jason. How about it, are you willing to take a chance? Remember, you think you're right, so you've got nothing to lose. All I want is a promise you'll listen. Have I got it?

Jason: Sure. I don't think you'll find any proof. I'm not afraid to have you look.

Matt: All right, then. I'll meet you here in a week.

> *Unfortunately, Matt has had to suggest this evidence. The maneuver may still work, however.*

> *Now the rules are set. Through careful argument Matt has a chance to persuade his friend.*

31. To See Or Not To See

Julie: Did you see where they convicted the guy who owned the sex shops?

Diana: No. What was it about?

Julie: Well, he was selling all sorts of sex aids and stuff. You know, vibrators and whatnot, and the cops came and arrested him for selling and displaying obscene material.

Diana: You're Kidding! And was he convicted?

Julie: yes. You sound like you don't approve.

Diana: I think it's incredible that someone should be convicted of that in our day and age. What has he done wrong?

> *Good. Julie is now forced to answer the first real question.*

Julie: Well, at the least he sold obscene stuff; that's illegal so he should be arrested.

Diana: Why should selling the stuff be illegal?

> *This is the fallacy of begging the question. If he has done nothing wrong he should not be arrested.*
The correct response. The reason Julie gave (that it is illegal so he should be arrested) is treated like a conclusion.

Julie: It's offensive to many people.

Diana: So what? Should everything that offends people be illegal? Lots of people are still offended by two-piece bathing suits.

> *Diana has neatly picked out Julie's principle— things offensive to many people should be illegal. Diana immediately thinks of an example that will not please Julie.*

Julie: That's different. It's just a question of style.

> *Julie is now bound, by the Principle of Similar Cases, to show a relevant difference between bathing suits and vibrators.*

Diana: Style? That just means popularity. Why do things have to be accepted? There was a time, you know, when women were arrested for wearing bikinis.

Julie: But now they're not. As tastes change we become more liberal. That's fine.

Diana: I don't understand what you're getting at.

> *Excellent. Diana is confused, and instead of pretending to understand she tells Julie.*

Julie: I don't think everything should be allowed. The tough part is how to figure where to stop. O.K., so we allow bikinis. But should we allow stores to sell vibrators? What about whips and chains? The only way to get it all straightened out is to have fuzzy laws. Then when someone is arrested we can let the courts try it.

Diana: That just comes down to letting the minority set standards for the majority.

> *This is not at all what Julie said. It is the fallacy of straw man, a distortion.*

Julie: So? What's wrong with that?

> *Julie has missed the fallacy, but she has been quick enough to question Diana's claim. All too often we never question the obvious.*

Diana: I don't know. I guess I never thought about it.

Julie: Standards have to be set. The way we set up our government is letting one group lead us. That's democracy.

Diana: No there's a difference. Wait a minute, let me think... [*After a minute.*] Look, the people who convicted the guy were not elected, they were just chosen as a jury, right?

Julie: Right. so what?

Diana: Well, now. Suppose you and I and a couple of our friends had been on the jury. None of us is bothered by the stuff he was selling. You may approve of censorship, but you don't really care about vibrators. Correct?

Julie: That's right. Personally that equipment doesn't bother me.

Diana: So, if we were on the jury he wouldn't have been convicted. We would at least have kept him from a guilty verdict, right?

Julie: I suppose so, but what are you getting at?

Diana: Just this—his conviction has nothing to do with right and wrong, good and bad. He was unlucky to have a conservative jury. There is no justice here, just luck. I think that stinks.

Julie: When you put it that way I have to agree. But I still feel there should be some limits. And anyway, isn't the whole jury system a question of luck?

Diana: I guess so, to a certain extent. But in this case the jury had to decide if there was a crime at all. I think that's what happens when we try to legislates taste.

> *A valuable move. Taking a minute to think can make an amazing difference. No one ever said an argument cannot be stopped for a think-break.*

> *Diana carefully gets Julie's agreement at each step. This will prevent Julie from complaining later.*

> *Julie knows she is caught. But she remembers her position and wisely returns to it.*

32. Essaying A Service

Robbie: Hey, Claire, where you hurrying off to?

Claire: [*Looks around to make sure she's not overheard.*] Well, actually, I've got to get over to the essay service to pick up something they did for me.

Robbie: [*Loudly.*] You're going to an essay service!?!

Claire: Quiet! Yeah, I am. So what?

Robbie: Well, it's wrong, that's what.

> *Robbie would have done better had he first asked Claire why she was doing it.*

> *See. Now Robbie is defending.*

Claire: What's so wrong about it?

Robbie: It's cheating, Claire; that's wrong.

> *This actually begs the question since it's really another way of saying it's wrong.*

Claire: It's not cheating. It's creative time management.

Robbie: That's BS. And if it's not cheating how come you whispered when you talked about it?

> *Claire should have kept Robbie on the defense, but she didn't.*

> *Good. Now Robbie's questioning. He's also pointing up an important discrepancy between words and behavior.*

Claire: C'mon! Everybody does it, you know that.

Robbie: I don't do it, and all I know is that it's cheating.

Claire: [*Sounding stressed.*]

> *The fallacy of ad populum is often used in this situation.*

> *Good. Robbie himself proved to be the counter-example.*

> *This is a change of subject*

You're just being a rule-monger. You don't follow every little rule.

Robbie: That's not the point. This rule is for you. The reason you're in school is to learn, if someone writes your essays for you, then you're not learning anything.

Claire: I'm learning plenty. Just because I don't do everything doesn't mean I'm not.

Robbie: You sure didn't learn anything about this assignment. And, besides being unfair to you, it's not fair to everyone else.

Claire: What's it got to do with anyone else?

Robbie: Well, look, I don't have as much money as you have, so I have to write my stuff, meet deadlines, and so on. Just because you're loaded, you don't have to. That's not fair.

Claire: I also get to drive to school because I can afford a car. Is that unfair?

Robbie: You know that's not the same; driving isn't cheating. what about the class curve? If you've got some unemployed Ph.D. writing an undergrad essay for you everyone else is going to look bad. You'll get an 'A' and we'll look like simpletons.

Claire: Well, I don't know. [*More stress is starting to show.*] Why are you making a federal case out of it?

Robbie: Because cheating effects us all. You think it's only got to do with you but...

Claire: All right, all right. So I'm cheating a little. What's the big deal. I was so stressed out... [*Tears show in Claire's eyes.*]

> *from what Claire is doing to what Robbie does or doesn't do.*

> *Good. Robbie didn't bite.*

> *Robbie has now presented a position which, given how things were going is may not be a bad idea.*

> *Good—if you don't understand, ask.*

> *A good response. Notice how the example addresses the Principle Principle and uses the Principle of Similar Cases.*

> *Robbie shows the difference between the two, and then quickly moves on.*

> *This argument refers to Robbie's own interest in the matter, and this makes it stronger.*

> *Claire does not have a good answer and would like to beg off the argument.*

> *Robbie is staying with what worked.*

> *OK, so Robbie has an admission, but that's not the most important information that was passed.*

Robbie: Hey, yeah, don't worry, I'm not going to report you. But what do you mean about the stress.

Claire: Oh, it was just everything as once. My mother...

> *Good. Robbie's paying attention to what might really be going on.*

The argument has moved from Claire's tactical defenses to a deeper level. Now Robbie might be able to both understand why Claire did what she did, as well as get a commitment that she won't do it again. Claire might benefit from sharing with Robbie, and even get some help in dealing with her stress.

33. To Therapy Or Not To Therapy

Ralph: Hey, Jerry, why the hang dog look?

Jerry: Oh, I don't know...

Ralph: C'mon, Jer, you're usually the happiest guy around.

Jerry: Well, you haven't been around me for some time. Not since my marriage went on the rocks.

Ralph: Your marriage? Oh, gee, that's awful. You and Fran used to be so happy. What happened?

Jerry: Who knows? You know women. One day everything's fine, the next they're telling you you're unfeeling, out of touch, and generally a slob.

Ralph: So, have you split? I mean, if I'm not intruding.

Jerry: No, not yet. But Fran says if I don't agree to counseling we're finished.

Ralph: And you don't want to?

Jerry: You're damned straight I don't want to. That's all bull.

Ralph: Well, what do you mean, "bull"?

Jerry: [*Looks at Ralph askance.*] Hell, what am I supposed to do. Go

> *Jerry doesn't know it, but the disagreement has begun.*

> *Ralph will try to get as much information from Jerry as he can. This is important to prevent wasting time and following false paths.*

> *Jerry hasn't really added anything yet.*

in and tell some guy my problems because my wife's unhappy?

Ralph: Well, lots of couples in trouble go into counseling.

Jerry: Well, I'm not lots of couples. Besides, Fran wants us to see this woman. Can't you just see it? The two of them ganging up on me, showing me it's all my fault.

Ralph: Hey, a good therapist doesn't let anybody talk about blame. They don't take sides. They focus on the two of you communicating.

Jerry: Oh, yeah, "communicating"— the word of the year.

Ralph: Well, it's really important in a relationship, don't you think?

Jerry: Hell, I communicate plenty. You know me, Ralph, I never shut up.

Ralph: Yeah, but I don't think yakking and communicating are exactly the same thing.

Jerry: [Says nothing, but looks miserable.]

Ralph: [Sympathetically.] Look, if there was something wrong with your car you'd go to a mechanic, right?

Jerry: Sure.

Ralph: And if you suddenly got terrible pains in your gut, you'd go to a doctor, right?

Jerry: [Slightly suspicious.] Yeah, I guess so.

Ralph: [Really careful now.] And, if you started acting crazy and having nightmares or something you might even go to a shrink, right?

Jerry: I don't know...

Ralph: Of course you would, you're no fool. If something's wrong you find an expert and get help.

> *Jerry didn't go for the ad populum, even though it was a fair comment.*

> *Let's see if Ralph drops it.*

> *Good, Ralph is following Jerry's lead. In a sensitive argument like this one you mustn't push too hard.*

> *Now Ralph has asked a question. Maybe he'll get somewhere.*

> *Not all statements happen with words.*

> *Ralph is going to try to get Jerry to see things in a different light.*

> *Jerry has agreed with Ralph's hidden principle, see an expert. Now Ralph needs to test it further.*

> *Ralph is pushing the principle.*

> *Jerry begins to see where this is going.*

> *Now Ralph has stated his principle and we'll see what Jerry does.*

Jerry: [*Reluctantly.*] Well, yeah, I guess so.

Ralph: So, if your marriage is in trouble you go to a marriage counselor, don't you?

Jerry: It's just so damned scary. I mean, I'm not good at exposing my so-called "inner self.". What if I do and Fran doesn't like what she sees?

Ralph: Hey, guy, you're right. What she's asking you to do is scary, and it's O.K. to be scared. But, remember what's at stake: You and Fran staying together.

Jerry: Yeah. [*Pause*] I do love her, you know.

Ralph: Then it's worth a little risk, isn't it? Hell, you might even be less of a jerk when you're finished.

Jerry: [*Takes a mock swing at Ralph.*] Ha! You'll still make me look like an amateur.

> *Suggesting that Jerry would be a fool to disagree is a form of ad baculum, but we'll let it pass.*

> *Jerry's agreement here is crucial.*

> *This applies the principle to Jerry's case.*

> *Note that Jerry did not actually assent to the principle. In some cases it might be important to get confirmation, but not with a subject like this.*

> *Ralph accepts Jerry's implicit agreement, and moves to a deeper level with a different argument.*

> *Now they're talking about what's really going on.*

> *Ralph wraps up the point, and adds a joke to soften the mood.*

34. Section III Review

Question

A. Create a commentary on the following dialogue in the style of this section.

Judy: Mark, I really can't believe you're one of those people who thinks everyone should own a gun.

Mark: Do you know what would happen if the government took our guns away?

Judy: Fewer people would get murdered?

Mark: No, *more!* Citizens would not be able to protect themselves, criminals would know that. They'd feel safe and break into every home they wanted to. Soon we'd all have to live in barred houses and be terrified to walk out at night. After that it would only be a matter of time before even daylight wasn't safe.

Judy: Oh, don't be so dramatic—you've got no way of knowing if that scary story will happen.

Mark: I know that the right to bear arms is esssential to a democracy.

Judy: Then how come the first thing the U.S. army did when it wanted to put a democracy back in Haiti was call in all the guns? Huh? Answer me that?

Well, the wrong people had the guns. If all the citizens had guns, then the dictator could never have stayed in power. There would have been a revolution and he'd have been thrown out.

You mean there would have been a bloody civil war and one of the two sides, the one with the most guns, would have won. You think everything can be solved by guns. Just go out and shoot and that's the end of it. If two kids are fighting over a toy, then one of them should get a gun and ...

Hey, just a minute! That's ridiculous and you know it. All I'm saying is that guns are blamed for a lot more things than they deserve to be.

Maybe, but do you really think the way to stop violence is to arm every-body? What if there were really strong penalties for carrying unregistered guns? Wouldn't than keep the criminals at bay?

Oh, yeah, some judge'll slap them on the hand and let them go, that's all.

I know, but what if they didn't? What if there were no choice? Mandatory two years with no parole for carrying an unregistered weapon?

I don't know. I mean they haven't...

Yeah, but they could. If we could find a way of controlling the criminals and have fewer guns wouldn't that be best?

Mark: Sure, but target shooters still have a right to...

B.   As a general habit, you should try to occasionally observe arguments from a distance. Sometimes, when in a group that is arguing about something, sit back and pay attention to the flow of the argument. Notice who is listening, who is changing the subject, who is responding to arguments. Listen for fallacies, equivocations, fudge words, and inconsistencies. Arguing well is an art, and it rquires patience and practice as well as study.

Answer

Here are my comments on this argument. Please understand that different people may notice different things when following a dispute.

4. This is a classic slippery slope fallacy. It assumes that once the first step is taken, every will follow inexorably. In fact, there are many other scenarios.

5. Judy has caught the fallacy, but notice that she did not give a counter-argument, just a denial.

6. Mark is changing the subject so he won't have to defend his predictions.

7. Judy didn't notice, but she did use a good counterexample. If Mark's principle is that guns are essential to democracy, why, in Haiti, did they seem to prevent it?

9. Judy is using a straw man fallacy to exaggerate Mark's position.

10. Good. Mark caught the move and called Judy on it. Now, if Judy is smart, she'll notice a slight moderation in his position. This might signal an opportunity.

11. Now Judy is asking a question—that hasn't happened much in this dispute. She's offering an alternative to see if Mark might negotiate.

12. Mark responds with a *non sequitor*, a change of subject.

13. Good. Judy gets him right back to her question.

15. Mark is weakening. Judy interrupts to press home her point.

16. Mark seems to agree, but then changes the subject. Judy's strategy at this point should be to agree to some leeway for target shooters, and then recap her position for Mark. At that point she'll see if he will hold to his agreement.

35. Going Further

The best way to hone your argument skills to is argue, especially when you are in situations where not too much is at stake. This allows you to listen carefully and pay attention to what you are doing when you are not dangerously involved. You can also take advantage of situations when others are arguing and you can sit back and listen. Try to spot fallacies and mistakes; notice who is listening and who is not; identify times when the subject changes and no one notices. By doing this you are training yourself to listen and react when in a safe situation.

Many colleges and universities offer courses in argumentation. These are frequently listed under the heading of "Critical Thinking" or "Informal Logic". Contact your local campus and inquire about these courses in their Adult Education or regular programs. Do try to make sure that the instructor is qualified in the field, and not just someone assigned to the course. These courses provide you with tools for arguing as well as partners to argue with.

There are a multitude of books containing valuable information about creative and effective ways to argue. I will only recommend a few, several at each of the various levels of expertise you might want to explore.

Basic Material

Among popular books relating to argument I recommend the following.

Capaldi, Nicholas. *The Art of Deception*. Prometheus.

Huff, Darrel. *How To Lie With Statistics*. Norton.

Fisher, Roger & Ury, William. *Getting to Yes*. Houghton Mifflin.

Interesting Textbooks

If you go to your local library and search the area where books on Critical Thinking and Informal Logic are shelved, you will find many choices. Here are a few, but there are many others.

Johnson, Ralph, and Blair, J. Anthony. *Logical Self-Defense*. McGraw-Hill.

Govier, Trudy. *A Practical Study of Argument* Wadsworth.

Groarke, Leo, and Christopher W. Tindale. 2003. *Good reasoning matters! : a constructive approach to critical thinking*. 23rd ed. Toronto ; New York: Oxford University Press.

Tindale, Christopher W. *Rhetorical Argumentation : Principles of Theory and Practice*. Thousand Oaks, Calif.: Sage Publications, 2004.

Heavy Duty

The field of Argumentation Theory has been changing and developing dramatically over the past twenty-five years. It has become multi-disciplinary and draws on research, not only from Philosophy, but from Communication Theory, Sociology and Psychology as well. The following books, intended for experts in the field, are extremely dense and technical, but advanced readers might find them of interest.

Cox, J.R., & Willard, C.A. *Advances in Argumentation Theory & Research*. Southern Illinois Univ Press.

Eemeren, Frans. H. van, Rob Grootendorst, and Arnolda Francisca Snoeck Henkemans. 1996. *Fundamentals of argumentation theory : a handbook of historical backgrounds and contemporary developments*. Mahwah, N.J.: L. Erlbaum.

Gilbert, Michael A. 1997. *Coalescent argumentation*. Mahwah, N.J.: Lawrence Erlbaum Associates.

Hall, Lavinia. ed., Negotiation: Strategies for Mutual Gain. Sage.

Johnson, Ralph, and Blair, J. Anthony, eds. *New Essays in Informal Logic.* [Available from the Department of Philosophy, University of Windsor, Windsor, Ontario N9B 3P4.]

Also in this category are the scholarly *journals Informal Logic, Argumentation, Argumentation & Advocacy,* and *Philosophy & Rhetoric.*

Professional Development & Talks

Through my business, Paradox Communications, 70 Withrow Avenue, Toronto, Canada M4K 1C9, I offer workshops and seminars for businesses and groups, give talks to meetings and clubs, and address social and professional functions. Depending on the needs of the client, these range from a lighthearted overview of some problems in argument to in-depth training in the techniques of argument and critical discussion. Find out more at,

www.howtowinanargument.com

Index